In Step With God

101 devotional walks through the Bible

Richard Littledale

Copyright © 2024 Richard Littledale

30 29 28 27 26 25 24   7 6 5 4 3 2 1

First published 2024 by Authentic Media Limited,
PO Box 6326, Bletchley, Milton Keynes, MK1 9GG.
authenticmedia.co.uk

The right of Richard Littledale to be identified as the Author of this Work
has been asserted in accordance with the
Copyright, Designs and Patents Act 1988.

All rights reserved.
No part of this publication may be reproduced, stored
in a retrieval system, or transmitted in any form or by any means,
electronic, mechanical, photocopying, recording or otherwise, without
the prior permission of the publisher or a licence permitting restricted
copying. In the UK such licences are issued by the Copyright Licensing
Agency, 5th Floor, Shackleton House, 4 Battle Bridge Lane, London SE1 2HX.

British Library Cataloguing in Publication Data
A catalogue record for this book is available from the British Library.
ISBN: 978-1-78893-326-1
978-1-78893-327-8 (e-book)

Scripture quotations taken from
The Holy Bible, New International Version Anglicised
Copyright © 1979, 1984, 2011 Biblica
Used by permission of Hodder & Stoughton Ltd, an Hachette UK company.
All rights reserved.
'NIV' is a registered trademark of Biblica
UK trademark number 1448790.

Cover design by Rina Pal (Lizaa)
Printed and bound by CPI Group (UK) Ltd, Croydon, CR0 4YY

Dedication

To the people of Prince's Drive Baptist Church, Colwyn Bay, who welcomed me when my footsteps brought me to their door.

Contents

	Preface	ix
	Introduction	1
	Choosing Your Footwear	3
	A Prayer for the Journey	7
	How to Use This Book	9
Walk 1	God Walks in the Garden	11
Walk 2	Adam and Eve Walk from the Garden	13
Walk 3	Cain Begins the Longest Walk	15
Walk 4	All Aboard	17
Walk 5	Enoch's Seamless Walk	19
Walk 6	On Cutting Ties	21
Walk 7	Hagar's Lonely Road	23
Walk 8	Abram's Steep Climb	25
Walk 9	Jacob's Ladder	27
Walk 10	Jacob Walks to Meet Esau	29
Walk 11	Joseph Walks into a Trap	31
Walk 12	Joseph's Brothers Walk into the Throne Room	33
Walk 13	Balaam's Ass	35
Walk 14	Jochebed's Triumph	37
Walk 15	Moses Flees to Midian	39
Walk 16	Moses and the Burning Bush	41
Walk 17	Moses Goes Up the Mountain	43
Walk 18	Moses Walks Down the Mountain	45
Walk 19	Hur and Aaron Step Up	47
Walk 20	Rahab Walks Up to the Roof	49
Walk 21	Joshua Walks Across the Riverbed	51
Walk 22	The Trumpeters Walk the Walls	53

Walk 23	An Angel Walks into a Winepress	55
Walk 24	Gideon Walks by Night	57
Walk 25	Samson's Last Steps	59
Walk 26	Ruth Walks to a Strange Land	61
Walk 27	Ruth Walks in the Fields	63
Walk 28	Hannah Walks to the Temple	65
Walk 29	Hannah Walks Back to the Temple	67
Walk 30	Samuel Walks into the Temple	69
Walk 31	Samuel Walks to an Anointing	71
Walk 32	David Walks into Battle	73
Walk 33	Elijah Walks Away from God	75
Walk 34	Elijah Walks to Heaven	77
Walk 35	A Man Walks to the Door	79
Walk 36	Naaman Walks to the River	81
Walk 37	Four Lepers Take a Midnight Walk	83
Walk 38	Nehemiah Walks into the Throne Room	85
Walk 39	Nehemiah Paces the Walls	87
Walk 40	A Queen on a Mission	89
Walk 41	A Walk Back to Job	91
Walk 42	A Walk Together	93
Walk 43	Daniel's Friends Walk in the Furnace	95
Walk 44	Daniel Walks from the Lions' Den	97
Walk 45	Hosea Walks the Walk of Shame	99
Walk 46	Jonah Walks Away	101
Walk 47	Jonah Walks to a Sulking Spot	103
Walk 48	The Magi Walk Away from Bethlehem	105
Walk 49	Walking to Egypt	107
Walk 50	People Walk to the River	109
Walk 51	Jesus Walks Down to the Water	111
Walk 52	Jesus Walks into the Wilderness	113
Walk 53	Peter Walks on Water	115

Walk 54	Jesus Walks into the Temple	117
Walk 55	The Dead Walk	119
Walk 56	Levi Walks After Jesus	121
Walk 57	Jesus Walks into a Synagogue	123
Walk 58	A Demoniac Walks Home	125
Walk 59	Jairus Walks Through the Crowd	127
Walk 60	Walking Across the Threshold	129
Walk 61	Up the Mountain with Jesus	131
Walk 62	Bartimaeus Follows On	133
Walk 63	Jesus Walks into the Garden	135
Walk 64	Simon Walks Beneath a Cross	137
Walk 65	Mary Walks to Elizabeth	139
Walk 66	Mary and Joseph Walk to Bethlehem	141
Walk 67	The Shepherds Walk Down from the Hills	143
Walk 68	Walking in a Panic	145
Walk 69	Jesus Walks from the Brink	147
Walk 70	A Widow's Son Walks	149
Walk 71	A Meal Interrupted	151
Walk 72	The Twelve Walk Out on a Mission	153
Walk 73	Martha Walks from the Kitchen	155
Walk 74	One of Ten Walks Back	157
Walk 75	Zaccheus Takes a Short Walk	159
Walk 76	Strangers Walk Off with a Donkey	161
Walk 77	A Man Walks with a Water Jar	163
Walk 78	Peter and John Walk to the Garden	165
Walk 79	A Strange Walk to Emmaus	167
Walk 80	Nathanael Walks with Philip	169
Walk 81	Nicodemus Takes a Night-time Walk	171
Walk 82	Jesus Walks Off Grid	173
Walk 83	Walking with a Bed	175
Walk 84	Walking Away from Jesus	177

Walk 85	Martha Walks with Jesus	179
Walk 86	A Short Walk for Judas	181
Walk 87	Mary Walks in the Garden	183
Walk 88	Mary Walks from the Garden	185
Walk 89	The Disciples Walk to Breakfast	187
Walk 90	Philip Walks to a Crossroads	189
Walk 91	Peter Walks Off for a Power Nap	191
Walk 92	Saul Walks into Damascus	193
Walk 93	Ananias Takes a Brave Walk	195
Walk 94	Rhoda Walks to the Door	197
Walk 95	Paul and Barnabas Walk Separate Ways	199
Walk 96	Paul Walks Away from the Border	201
Walk 97	The Apostles Walk from Jail	203
Walk 98	Paul Walks Next Door	205
Walk 99	A Walk on the Quayside	207
Walk 100	A Prisoner Walks Free	209
Walk 101	A Walk Home	211
Walk 102		213
	Postscript: A Walk Continued	215
	Notes	221

Preface

In the National Air and Space Museum in Washington, DC, there is a footprint. It is not a trail of prints, nor even a pair, just a cast of one single print, the ridges on the tread cut deeply for all to see. It is a cast of the first impression made by a single human foot on another world – the surface of the moon. Somehow the whole multi-billion-dollar story of the race to space, and the costly endeavour to get there, is all etched into that one single footprint. In it, a story both vast and complex of the quest for knowledge and humankind's insatiable curiosity is all writ small in that one shape. That story, we feel, is our story.

Human beings have been marking the surface of this particular planet with their footprints ever since they first existed. The marks traced by footsteps across the surface of the earth, like the lines of ageing on a face, tell a story between them. In many ways, it is the story of the human race. Rebecca Solnit, in her history of walking, *Wanderlust*, puts it like this:

> Walking has been one of the constellations in the starry sky of human culture, a constellation whose three stars are the body, the imagination, and the wide-open world.[1]

Christians have often found walking to be an aid to prayer and contemplation, as the rhythms of body and soul fall into step with one another. In the fourth century Basilica of St Reparus in Orleansville, Algeria, there is an etched labyrinth with the words 'Santa Ecclesia' etched at its centre. It was doubtless used as an aid to prayer, as was a bigger and more famous example at Chartres Cathedral. Many medieval monasteries included a cloister in their design, where their residents could walk and pray without ever leaving the confines of their sacred community. At their height, the great pilgrim trails criss-crossing Europe were like the vascular system of Christianity, carrying prayerful pilgrims to and fro. Christians have always found a certain solace in placing one faithful footstep in front of the other.

Of course, people are always on the move in the Bible. Sometimes they sail in ships, sometimes ride on a horse or a donkey and, on at least one occasion, ride in a flaming chariot which hauled them into the skies. For the most part, though, the journeys are on foot. In the pages which follow, I have assembled a collection of them. Of course, there are hundreds of them, but I have selected 101 here. Some are long journeys, like Ruth's from one country to another. Others are remarkably short, like little Samuel's walk from one room in the temple to another to deliver his dreadful message. Some walks ascend the heights and others descend into the valleys. Our walkers will ascend mountains and gangplanks, and cross everything from seas and rivers to international borders.

I hope that you will find they make for good company.

Introduction

Running was never my thing. Unlike famous athlete and missionary Eric Liddell, who believed that God had made him fast, the same could not be said of me. At school, I was the pariah of PE lessons, and always ended up on the team of whoever lost the toss at the start of the lesson. For a brief spell, I became something of an enthusiast for cross-country running. However, it was a shallow enthusiasm. Me and my fellow runners were simply those who preferred not to participate in team games, where we inevitably let the side down. Instead, we would meander round the roads and lanes on the appointed route, before puffing and blowing through the school gate with a great display of exertion for the teacher's benefit.

Many years later, I was just starting a sabbatical from ministry, and felt inspired by the running feats of my eldest son. To his (and my own) amazement, I signed up for a 10km run, and started training in earnest. A few weeks into it, I picked up an injury, and had to seek medical advice. One thing led to another, and one appointment led to another, until at last I came face to face with a kindly doctor who broke what he thought might be bad news to me.

'Mr Littledale,' he announced gravely, 'I am sorry to say that running is not the sport for you.'

I could have hugged him! In the ensuing years I took up cycling. I started with short local rides around London's Bushy Park and ended up going as far as the 100-mile RideLondon event.

Life then took another turn, as circumstances dramatically changed. After many years of illness, and many months of being nursed at home, my wife succumbed to cancer in late 2017. As I began to find my life again, I adopted a rescue dog – a beautiful brindled lurcher called Ginny. She became my constant companion, and needed at least two walks every day. Cycle shoes were replaced by walking shoes, and together we explored near and far. Walking became a kind of therapy to me, a sort of physical antidote to the emotional pain.

When I was researching *Journey: The Way of the Disciple*,[2] it became apparent to me that there was much more to walking than simply putting one foot in front of the other. At a profound level, walking pace and thinking pace are linked. Not only that, but our understanding both of ourselves and of the landscape we traverse is transformed when we cross it in that particular way. We understand it and interact with it at a different level when we cross it on foot, rather than driving or riding through it, or flying over it. When we start walking *and* talking with God, walking itself becomes almost sacramental.

As I reflected on all of that, it dawned on me that people were walking with God long before pilgrimages or cloisters or labyrinths were invented. The first walk in God's presence was conducted by Humans 1.0 Adam and Eve; and followed by hundreds of others. What if we were to use *their* footsteps to help *us* traverse the biblical landscape? Maybe by falling in step with them, we would understand that biblical landscape better than if we flew over it with an overview or drove through it in a hurry. Going through the Bible at walking pace might provide us with the companionable encounter with its author for which our souls cry out.

All these factors, combined with a new phase of my life where I have time to slow things down long enough to walk, pray and listen more than ever before, have led to the writing of this book. Care to join me for a long walk?

Choosing Your Footwear

Many years ago, when I was a rather reluctant member of my local Scout troop, the kit list would come out every year ahead of the annual camp and would include a line calling for 'hiking boots or stout walking shoes'. I generally went down the hiking boots line, but always wondered what exactly might constitute a 'stout walking shoe'? Maybe it was something to do with the materials – leather rather than canvas. Maybe it was to do with the 'weight' and construction, or the tread? I suppose I shall never know now.

What are you going to wear for this shared journey of ours? Of course, you might wear anything from pink fluffy slippers to high-tech trainers while reading this. You might even choose to read it barefoot. One year, I conducted the Maundy Thursday communion service in my usual preaching suit . . . but with bare feet. It felt distinctly unnerving, but also gave me a new understanding of what it meant to stand on holy ground. Feeling the floor through my bare feet kept me grounded as never before. Week by week now, I worship in a church where the minister removes his shoes for the entirety of the worship. For him, it is not so much about holiness as about comfort. To him, a place where you kick off your shoes is a place where you feel at home, and he would like church to be that way.

Maybe what is called for here is not so much a choice of footwear, but a choice of gait.

Tread softly

It was W.B. Yeats who wrote in his poem 'He Wishes for the Cloths of Heaven' that you should 'Tread softly for you tread on my dreams'.[3] Treading softly means thinking carefully about where you place each footstep, as you might when approaching wildlife in the forest. Weigh each footstep cautiously in case you should snap a twig and scare your quarry away. Look down once in a while to make sure that you are not about to trip over a root nor step down into an unexpected hollow. Our journey will repay careful footsteps, I think.

Tread hopefully

Near where I used to live there was a ruined castle. It was not huge, but it had real character; its squat towers and cannon-scarred walls overlooked the landscape for miles around. Oddly, on the approach road to the castle, it was not possible to see it until the very last bend in the steep approach road. No matter how many times I visited, my heart would still quicken on coming around that last bend at the prospect of the sight which awaited me. It is the same with climbing the last few steps to a view of the sea or the brow of a hill. Our footsteps reflect on the outside the feelings we have inside. Ours should be a hopeful journey in the pages of this book too – anticipating a better view, perhaps, and sights to lift the spirits.

Tread with determination

When I was little, my dad loved to walk. He had grown up on long country walks and youth hostelling and was keen to share both with his sons. The trouble was, he had very long legs and I only had short ones. Often was the time I could be found whingeing at the back of the line that it was 'too far'. I overcame it, though. With time, I learned simply to keep putting one foot in front of the other and enjoy the walk along the way. My father taught me to make the most of the sights as we went along, rather than allowing the whole walk to be dominated by a preoccupation with its end. The walk of faith is a long one, no matter whereabouts in your life you join it. To see it through will take determination and grit. Let's set out on this journey with a degree of determination in our step.

Tread companionably

In my latter years as a pastor, I found that more and more of my meetings with members of my church were *walking* meetings. Somehow, the movement of our feet kept the conversation moving too. Being beside each other, rather than face-to-face, often made for an easier and more companionable conversation. To walk in company can be a lovely thing. My walks every morning with my lurcher, Ginny, come rain or shine, are some of the sweetest moments of my day. Our journey over all the pages which follow is a shared one. You and I take this journey together. However, there will be others reading this book and turning the pages at exactly the same time. Try to think of them as you make this journey. You may find their unseen company quite a help!

A Prayer for the Journey

In centuries gone by, pilgrims on the great pilgrimage route from France to Santiago de Compostela in Spain would stop at the Abbey of Roncesvalles for a service of blessing and prayer before they continued. Like our pilgrim predecessors, we do the same before we embark on our journey together.

Dear God

Ahead of us lies a journey in the company of your saints, both great and small.

In faith and hope we plant our footsteps in theirs, trusting that the God who guided them will do the same for us.

As you provided strength, hope and companionship to them, do it for us too, we pray.

It is our prayer that through these walks we might travel not only towards you, but with you.

Be our light in darkness, our shelter on the way and the hope before us, we pray.

Amen.

How to Use This Book

The words in this book are intended to form only one part of a spiritual exercise. Ideally, they should be combined with a walk each day. It doesn't have to be a long walk. It might be around the corner to the shops or down to the bottom of the garden. Then again, if you are on holiday, it might be a walk up the nearest hill or along the beach. You don't have to combine words and walking, of course, but I believe it will pay dividends if you do. The walks are written in the order in which they appear in the Bible. Of course, you can read them in any order, but you may find that reading them this way helps to connect the wider story of Scripture together. If possible, try to read this book in the morning before you walk anywhere, even if that walk is only from the front door to the car. That way, you can turn your thoughts into prayers and your prayers into paces as you head out into the day. Don't worry, the chapters are short, so reading them won't delay your journey. That said, they might change it a little. I certainly hope they will.

Walk 1

God Walks in the Garden

 Then the man and his wife heard the sound of the LORD God as he was walking in the garden in the cool of the day, and they hid from the LORD God among the trees of the garden. But the LORD God called to the man, 'Where are you?' He answered, 'I heard you in the garden, and I was afraid because I was naked; so I hid.'

Gen. 3:8–10

To me, there is something special about an evening walk. Somehow, the world is that little bit stiller, and you can absorb the sights, sounds and smells more than you can in the full busyness of the daytime. When I first came to faith, I loved to attend church both morning and evening as I learned about my new-found Saviour. That said, I found the evenings extra special. Most weeks, I would leave the house far too early and take a very long route around – just so that I had time to walk and pray and quieten my heart before worship. I miss those walks.

Our passage today contains the first walk in the entire Bible. Unusually it is not man, woman or child who is doing the walking. It is God himself. Here he comes, like a friendly neighbour taking a walk through the neighbourhood of an evening and stopping to chat over the garden fence. Perhaps he might ask the occupants of the garden how their day had been, or maybe how the things they had planted were growing? Sadly, it was not to be that way.

Often there are moments in all our lives when the one thing we want more than anything else is for God to swing by and ask us how we are doing. We feel like the proverbial tree in the forest, falling with no one to hear the sound that it makes. Does God even *know* what we are going through? It is a cry repeated many times in the most anguished of the psalms, where the writer cries out for some recognition of his plight.

How tragic that on this particular occasion things had got so messed up that these two people – chips off the old block and fashioned in his image – felt like the best response to God's arrival was to run and hide. All those old medieval paintings of Adam and Eve peering out coyly from the foliage don't quite capture it, do they? Adam and Eve are not coy, they are terrified. How do you hide from someone who sees everywhere?

Maybe you are having the type of day today when you feel the need to hide from God. Perhaps you can't put your finger on exactly why you feel that way. Then again, you might be like Adam and Eve, knowing full well what the problem is and feeling very exposed by it. To you, to me, and to all his children, God comes walking by today. Before our journey goes any further, why not step out from behind that bush and talk to him?

Prayer

> Dear God, often I have smiled at those old pictures of Adam and Eve, looking like naughty schoolchildren caught in the act. I'm not smiling today, though, because I think I know how they feel. I know I have done something that I should not have done. Not only that, but I know you are fully aware of it and I dare not look you in the eye. Please God, let your Holy Spirit nudge me in your direction today, that I might come out of hiding. Amen.

Walk 2

Adam and Eve Walk from the Garden

> The LORD God made garments of skin for Adam and his wife and clothed them. And the LORD God said, 'The man has now become like one of us, knowing good and evil. He must not be allowed to reach out his hand and take also from the tree of life and eat, and live for ever.' So the LORD God banished him from the Garden of Eden to work the ground from which he had been taken.
>
> *Gen. 3:21–23*

I was only 3 years old when Matt Monro released his single 'Walk Away' in 1967. I wasn't old enough to take it in, nor to be aware of the scandal that it caused because it told the story of an older man falling for a much younger woman. All the same, I find a lump in my throat every time as his mellifluous tones sing out the lyrics.[4] To me it is an anthem of regret, if ever there were one.

I can hear it now, as we read today's passage. Adam and Eve's awkward conversation with God as they hide in the bushes is over, and now they must live with the consequences. How heavy were their footsteps, I wonder, as they walked away from Eden? In that place there had been everything they had ever needed. They had lived free from disease and hardship of every kind. Yet now, as they cross the threshold of paradise, it will all be no more than a memory. Life as trial, rather than blessing, begins here.

Do you find it hard to walk away? I know I do. I remember walking away from a very exciting job offer. It would have offered the chance to live abroad for a while with my family and to interact with a congregation in one of the most cosmopolitan places on earth. It carried with it all sorts of possibilities. Unfortunately, it carried insurmountable obstacles too – and I had to turn it down. When my wife was very ill in hospital, I used to hate walking away from the ward at the end of visiting hours. With every step, my burden at the sense of leaving her would grow. Outside, the lights in all the windows would make the hospital building look like some vast ocean liner, and I felt like I had cast her adrift in it. Walking away is rarely easy.

If you are walking away from something today, know these two things. Firstly, know that God does not walk away from you. Secondly, know that he still cares for you. Did you notice that little sentence at the start of our reading today? Did you catch that moment when the Lord of the heavens and the earth became a tailor for a little while? It is a tender thing when God stops to make clothes for these two before they walk away from Eden for the last time. Of course, had they not eaten from the tree of the knowledge of good and evil they would not have needed them. Be that as it may, God will not have them chilly and exposed as they head out into the big wide world. In the midst of hardship, even when it is of our own making, God does not desert us.

Perhaps today is a day when you feel the need to walk away from something. It might be a habit which you need to break, or the bad company which encourages you to persist with it. It might be a really good job offer or a tempting opportunity which you know deep down in your heart is not for you. Whatever it is, remember the tailor-God of this passage who knows and who cares.

Prayer

Dear God, every footstep is leaden today, as I walk from this. Now, more than ever before, I feel the burden of simply putting one foot in front of the other. Please remind me that you are near – and that I do not walk on from here alone. Amen.

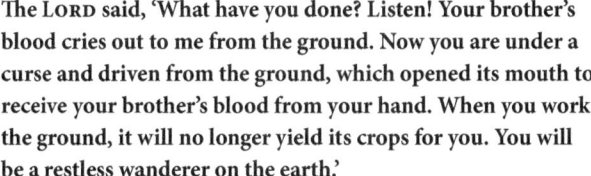

Cain Begins the Longest Walk

The LORD said, 'What have you done? Listen! Your brother's blood cries out to me from the ground. Now you are under a curse and driven from the ground, which opened its mouth to receive your brother's blood from your hand. When you work the ground, it will no longer yield its crops for you. You will be a restless wanderer on the earth.'

Gen. 4:10–12

I spent a lot of my student days in a theatre company, and I can remember a training workshop where the coach asked us to portray a state of emotion purely and simply by the way we walked. As we walked past her, depicting our chosen state, she shielded her eyes so that she could see each actor from the waist down only. She was looking carefully at gait, posture and the way we picked our feet up for each step. Were we 'telling a story' by the way we walked?

It is hard to make an exact judgement on the way that our character walks in today's passage. Is it anger, self-pity, regret or fear which dictates his footsteps, I wonder? Cain and his brother have brought offerings to God. Abel has brought the very best, and Cain just some of what he had. Abel's offering is accepted, Cain's is not, and Cain exacts a terrible vengeance by killing his brother.

After this God puts a 'mark' (v. 15) on Cain and sends him out. Often we have been so absorbed by puzzling about what the 'mark of Cain' might be that we fail to let the description of him as a 'restless wanderer' really sink in. What an awful thing to think that he would wander and wander without stopping, until at last he dropped. Although God assures him that no one will be able to take his life with impunity, it is still a heavy burden which he must bear. In the end, he settles in the 'land of *Nod*' (v. 16, my emphasis), the name of which means 'wandering' in Hebrew. His story features no more, beyond telling us the names of his children and their children.

Funnily enough, I can remember references to the 'land of Nod' when I was very little. It was a place where you went to sleep your worries away. Not so for Cain, I fear. His Land of Nod was a sorrowful place, where each footstep was heavier than the last, and no solace would be found.

If you are walking through that particular 'land of Nod' today, then may your journey be a short one. If, like Cain, your footsteps betray a mixture of anger, self-pity, regret and fear – then know that there is no place to which your feet can take you which is hidden from God. You may find it helpful to write down those things which are making you feel this way. There is no need to keep what you have written, and it is definitely only for your eyes and God's, rather than anybody else's. Having written them – why not take your piece of paper with you on a long walk today? Stamp or stride out the emotions written on there if you need to. You may well find that your walk on the homeward journey is very different to the outbound one. I hope so.

Prayer

> Lord, you know that I am so steamed up by these things going through my head that I don't even know what to call them. Are they angry thoughts, sorry thoughts . . . or something in-between? For now, I shan't worry about naming them. I will simply take them with me and let my feet help me with talking to you as I walk. Amen.

Walk 4

All Aboard

> The animals going in were male and female of every living thing, as God had commanded Noah. Then the LORD shut him in.
>
> *Gen. 7:16*

When I was growing up, our next-door neighbour loved cars. When my parents were spending their weekend on their knees weeding the garden, he was spending his flat on his back underneath his car, since he seemed to dismantle parts of it on a weekly basis. Often, his driveway would be a cluttered mess of cogs and bolts and containers of oil and grease. As hobbies go, it wasn't a particularly antisocial one. After all, he could have been ripping through timber with a screeching circular saw or practising the bagpipes!

I have often felt sorry for Noah's neighbours. After all, God hadn't told *them* about the forthcoming storm. They were in the dark. And yet – here was their crazy neighbour building a boat the size of a football stadium outside his house. As if that weren't bad enough, he then brought two of every kind of animal loping and hopping and crashing and crawling through the neighbourhood to board his boat. What a neighbour he was!

When at last the ark was complete, the time came to board it. After all the months of planning and construction, the time had come to fill this enormous vessel. Noah was charged with finding animals of every kind and ushering them onto the ark.

Before we get too taken in by that magnificent sight of the animals making their way into the ark, let's focus on the human walk. These eight human beings were walking up the gangplank as the last representatives of the human race. Behind them lay a world which, though flawed, was familiar.

Ahead of them lay a journey of uncertain duration or destination in the biggest homemade boat ever built. How long did that gangplank feel, I wonder? Did they face resolutely forward, or steal a wistful glance over their shoulders at everything they were leaving behind?

I'm sure you have had them too – those short walks which seem agonisingly long. It may have been the walk from the pavement through the door of a new job. It may have been the walk to the corner after waving goodbye to someone you love whom you will not see for a very long time. I can remember the long walk down the aisle after concluding my time as a particular church's minister. Of course, it was a route I had traced hundreds of times. On this occasion, though, it seemed twice as long, and carpeted the whole way with the memories of what had been.

If you are facing a short walk today which feels long – be sure that God will walk it with you. Did you notice that tender moment in our passage when it says that God closed the door behind Noah and his family? Here is a God with palms big enough to cup a universe or mould a planet, stopping to shut the door of what must have seemed to him a very tiny boat. The God who stretches as far as the edges of forever is right here at your side.

Prayer

> Dear God, today I am taking a deep breath because I have a hard walk to take. Walk it with me, please, that the journey might be shortened through the company I keep. Amen.

Walk 5

Enoch's Seamless Walk

Enoch walked faithfully with God; then he was no more, because God took him away.

Gen. 5:24

I have been fortunate enough to write this book from a small office on the coast of North Wales. From my vantage point up here, I can look out and see Liverpool Bay and the distant Irish Sea. On a clear day the view is divided into one-third of deep-blue sea, and two-thirds of sky above that. At the horizon line it is the palest, palest blue, on the verge of white, and as it climbs towards the top of my view, so it turns to a diluted cerulean blue. That is on a good day. On a bad day, sea and sky meld into one seamless curtain of gunmetal grey. On such a day I would be hard-pushed even to pick out the horizon as I look.

For most people, the horizon at the end of their lives can be seen from some distance away. The wisest plan for it, while others prefer not to talk about it. Of course, there will always be those caught unawares, taken down suddenly and unexpectedly, and for that there can be no planning. For Enoch, one of Adam's descendants, the whole thing went rather differently. After recording that he lived for an amazing 365 years, the writer of Genesis then writes that he simply 'was no more'.

Like my sea-sky-cloud days when all meld into one, Enoch's earthly walk simply became his heavenly one, without skipping a beat. Such was the closeness of his walk with God that it was impossible to tell the one state from the other. What a way to live your life, and what a legacy to leave behind.

On very rare occasions I have seen just such an end to people's lives. Their fellowship with God seems altogether unchanged by the proximity of death. Their natural trust in him and the breathed language of prayer seems to come as readily to them as it always did. They are as aware of God's presence in these darker days as they ever were in the full sun. When the time comes for a last breath to be drawn, it is not at all hard to believe that a simultaneous first breath is drawn in heaven. Their walk with God, like Enoch's, has been seamless.

Whatever today may bring, perhaps it would be an idea to concentrate on matching your pace with God, like trying to synchronise your breathing with a person beside you. Dwell on that picture of Enoch's faithful and continuous walk as you walk out into today.

Prayer

> Dear God, help me to match my walk with you as I head out into today, I pray. Like Enoch before me, help me to walk 'faithfully' with you, whatever that may look like. Amen.

Walk 6

On Cutting Ties

The LORD had said to Abram, 'Go from your country, your people and your father's household to the land I will show you.
'I will make you into a great nation,
 and I will bless you;
I will make your name great,
 and you will be a blessing.
I will bless those who bless you,
and whoever curses you I will curse;
and all peoples on earth
will be blessed through you.'
So Abram went, as the LORD had told him; and Lot went with him.

Gen. 12:1–4

We talked in a previous chapter about short walks which seem like long ones. I can remember one in particular in my own life. The year was 1987, and I was due to graduate that summer. At the time, I was engaged to be married to Fiona. We had a wedding date, but no job or home to go to. Over a period of weeks and through numerous means, God had confirmed to me that I should seek training for ordained ministry without further delay. This being so, my applications for other jobs had no place in the plan. My walk away from the University Careers Advisory Service, having cancelled all my job applications, was one which I shall never forget.

Apart from the names of his parents and the place of his birth, we know very little about Abram (or Abraham, as he would become) and his early life. What we *do* know is that people, place and land would have meant more to him than it does to us. These things were his anchors, they were the strands that bound his life together. For God to come to him at the age of 75 and ask him to cut all three was no small thing. I illustrated this once in church by cutting the ribbons which held three helium-filled balloons in place. They were labelled 'people', 'place' and 'land', and with one snip they floated all the way up to the high ceiling where nobody could reach them. It took me a long time, and a lot of effort, to get them down.

Perhaps the most remarkable word in today's entire passage is the monosyllable 'So'. Having been asked to make a change and take a personal risk of gargantuan proportions, Abram simply gets on and does it. This kind of decisiveness is one which we shall encounter on one of our subsequent walks with him, in Walk 8.

How do you fare when making such decisions? Some people find the thrill of it all to be energising. For my own part, I confess that I find it very daunting. I am writing this now in my little office on the North Welsh Coast. About nine months ago, God confirmed to me that the time had come to leave ordained pastoral ministry behind. Having done it all my working life, it was a shock to step away from it. I no longer have the status nor the responsibilities which once formed my daily life. My diary is alarmingly empty, and I am waiting for God to fill it. The command to 'up sticks' and leave is never an easy one to follow. That said, there are times when we can only be obedient to him by leaving the familiar behind.

Today is a good day to talk to God about the onward journey and how it feels. Reflect in his presence on the things you will leave behind and others which you may encounter.

Prayer

> Dear God, today I stand at a crossroads and look at the road ahead with you. What is out there, I wonder? Will the road rise or fall? Will it twist this way or that? Help me to remember today that whatever else I may leave behind, I do not leave you. Amen.

Walk 7

Hagar's Lonely Road

Early the next morning Abraham took some food and a skin of water and gave them to Hagar. He set them on her shoulders and then sent her off with the boy. She went on her way and wandered in the Desert of Beersheba.

Gen. 21:14

The description of that 'sinking feeling' has become the stock-in-trade of so many poor jokes that it is hard to take it seriously. However, there are journeys on which you embark with exactly that feeling. From the moment you take your first step on such a walk, you know that the last step will surely bring you to a less than happy place.

Hagar's was just such a walk. She had borne a child to Abraham since his wife, Sarah, was unable to do so. Since then, things had changed for Sarah and she was now a mother. As their two boys grew up, there was enmity between them. Sarah insisted that Abraham's rightful heir should have precedence, and that the other woman and her child should be sent packing. It falls to Abraham to send them on their way.

How heavy Hagar's footsteps must have been as Abraham and her former home receded in the distance. It was one thing to risk the unforgiving desert for herself, but to do so for a child was considerably worse. As an adult, she would have been all too aware of how their resources were diminishing, and their chances of survival with them. Like tens of thousands of refugee mothers in the centuries since, she could see that her deepest desire, to protect her child, was one which she could not fulfil.

Imagine what it must be like to hear all the sighs and all the sobs and all the heartfelt prayers of the whole world all at once. Of course, we cannot. In the cacophony of all that noise and woe, God picks out the sound of one mother weeping for one child in one corner of one country. If ever there were a picture of the attentiveness of God – this is it.

It might be a good idea to save your prayer today so that you can pray it on the move. It doesn't matter whether you are hiking along a mountain path or sauntering round the corner to the shops. It will still work. As you walk, ask God to make you acutely aware of some of the needs around about you. It might be the needs of the people in that farmhouse tucked away down at the bottom of the valley where you are walking. It might be the needs of the staff at the late-night off-licence which you pass by on your way to the shops. Whichever it is, ask God to help you pray.

Prayer

Dear God, I could never hear all the things you hear nor see all the things you see. I could neither bear it nor understand it. I ask, though, that as I walk today you make me aware of just some of the needs around me. I want to raise them up to you in prayer, just as the sound of Hagar's quiet tears came up to you once before. Amen.

Walk 8

Abram's Steep Climb

> Abraham took the wood for the burnt offering and placed it on his son Isaac, and he himself carried the fire and the knife. As the two of them went on together, Isaac spoke up and said to his father Abraham, 'Father?' 'Yes, my son?' Abraham replied. 'The fire and wood are here,' Isaac said, 'but where is the lamb for the burnt offering?'
>
> *Gen. 22:6–8*

There was a spring in his step – all four of them. The woolly and beautiful German Shepherd trotting along at my side liked to visit the vet. In fact, he pretty much liked to visit anywhere where people would appreciate his noble nature and ruffle his magnificent mane. The trouble is, I knew what was coming and he did not. With every footstep from the car to the doorway of the surgery, and from the doorway to the counter, and from the counter to the consulting room, I was aware that a horrid injection was on the way. Sure enough, when the moment came, he did his best to hide behind me, as he always did. Knowing what was coming made the journey so much harder for me than for him.

As with our previous walk at Abram's side, we see an admirable resolve to get on with the matter in hand. Despite the fact he has been told that his beloved son, Isaac, must perish, he gets up 'Early the next morning' (v. 3) to do what he has been told to do.

It is almost impossible to imagine the tension on that early morning walk. As the two of them climbed up the mountain, and the sun climbed higher in the sky, the boy's innocence and his father's terrible knowledge must have made for uneasy companions. Did Isaac ask question after question, like a child when they have an adult's undivided attention? Did Abram talk nervously about anything and everything in order to keep his mind from what awaited them at the end of the walk?

I wonder how many nervous walks I have made with God? I know for a fact that I made one at least once each Sunday for more than thirty years. I never strode towards a pulpit or lectern without an acute awareness of my unworthiness to occupy such a place. When I heard part way through those years that Charles Haddon Spurgeon, the 'Prince of Preachers' often had to be manhandled into his pulpit at the Metropolitan Tabernacle for the same reason, I felt slightly better about it. Without those nerves, I would have been filled with entirely the wrong kind of confidence. When somebody commented on how easily it all seemed to come to me, I assured them that the day I stopped being nervous about it would be the day that I stopped doing it.

Counterintuitive though it is, it might be a good idea to take a long hard look at those things which trouble you before you pray today. Don't let today's walk with God be like Isaac's with Abram, where neither would really discuss the matter in hand. Make a list, right now, of the things that are bothering you. Once you have done so, choose the top one, which will occupy your conversation with God today. You might not resolve it, nor even fully get round to explaining it, but you will have made a start.

Prayer

> Dear God, sometimes people talk about an 'elephant in the room', but that phrase won't do for what I've got here today. Elephants make me smile, with their bendy trunks and their colossal feet – but this thing does not. This thing is more like a cloud in the room than an elephant. It sits up there in the corner of my consciousness, brooding and blocking out the light. Please can we talk about it today? I've a feeling that just the sound of your voice will start to break up the cloud. Amen.

Walk 9

Jacob's Ladder

> Surely the Lord is in this place, and I was not aware of it.
> *Gen. 28:16*

Every once in a while, it does us good to have an 'oh-I-never-knew-that' moment, don't you think? I have been driving cars for more than thirty-six years, and yet I only recently discovered that there was a piece of information on the dashboard which I never knew was there. Next to the fuel pump symbol on any car there is a little arrow, pointing either to the nearside or offside of the car. Apparently, it is telling you on which side of the car the fuel tank is to be found. If you learn nothing else from this book, then you may at least find that small gem to be useful when you next visit a garage!

In today's verse, Jacob has started out on what will be a long and uncomfortable journey. After stealing his own brother's birthright, a rift has opened in the family which will take many years to heal. Jacob's mother has warned him that his brother, Esau, is out to exact revenge, and that he must flee for his life. Part way into his journey, Jacob stops as the sun goes down. Taking a stone as a pillow, he lies down to sleep. As he does so, he has a vision of a ladder stretching to heaven, with the angels climbing up and down it. God reminds him of the promises made to Jacob's father, and his father before him, about their future and God's abiding presence. For Jacob, this was his 'I-never-knew-that' moment, and it would help him on his way.

Let's dwell on that vision of his, for a moment. So far in this book we have looked at God walking in the garden, and God's people walking to and fro. Here is something different again, though. Here we are thinking about angelic footsteps, constantly making the journey between earth and heaven;

heaven and earth. It is fun to dwell on what sort of footsteps they might be. Would they be soft ones, so gentle that you could scarcely hear them on the ladder, or hefty ones, like a brickie carrying bricks up and down in his hod? Of course we do not know, and that is not the point anyway. The point which Jacob needed to understand was one which is important for us too. As far away as they might seem from each other, earth and heaven are very close. The angels (who are God's messengers) can as easily cross the gap between here and there as a person might climb up a stepladder to fetch something from the top shelf. Help is at hand.

On your walk today, please don't shut your eyes as Jacob did, or the results may be disastrous. Why not take a little time, though, to dwell on that image of the angels coming and going on the ladder to heaven? Just think, even as you can hear the sound of your own footsteps on the pavement, there are other silent footsteps between heaven and earth as God's messengers go about his business. Some are striding to the rescue, others are delivering a message here or a dream there, but they are busy.

Prayer

Dear God, like Jacob, I have often been so unaware of your presence. You have been busy doing wonderful things right under my nose and I never noticed them. Please make me more aware of them today, I pray. Amen.

Walk 10

Jacob Walks to Meet Esau

He himself went on ahead and bowed down to the ground seven times as he approached his brother. But Esau ran to meet Jacob and embraced him; he threw his arms around his neck and kissed him. And they wept.

Gen. 33:3–4

Leadership is a privilege. As a Christian leader, you get the inestimable privilege of helping people along the road that leads them to the greater things of God. Often, you are entrusted with their secrets, too – so that their burdens might be shared. There is a downside, though. As a leader, your successes may be very public, but so are your failures. An unguarded word here or a careless phrase there can undo months of hard work by you and others. I have made more of those mistakes than I care to remember. I can still recall how leaden were my footsteps as I made my way to a coffee shop to speak to someone whom I had offended. I would love to say that they had been oversensitive or had misinterpreted me. Neither would be true. My words had been careless and damaging, and I was expecting to consume a large slice of humble pie with my coffee.

There were all kinds of bad blood between Jacob and his brother, Esau. Years before, he had cheated him out of his birthright, and nothing had ever been the same again. Over time, they had gone their separate ways, and the stories of each had unfolded. Now, though, Esau is on his way with 400 men at his side, and there will be no avoiding him. Jacob has spent a restless night, famously wrestling with a mysterious figure. As dawn rises, anticipating trouble, he places his children and his household behind him for safety before the showdown. That done, he heads off to meet his estranged brother.

Oddly enough, I have often preached on this passage at weddings. As Jacob and Esau head towards each other like two gunfighters in a western, they each have their retinue with them. They bring baggage, both physical and emotional, to the encounter. This is true of every bride and groom as they approach their marriage. Each brings the successes and failures, the joys and sorrows and the scars of the past to this new union. Grace and love will help them to overcome all this.

As it turns out, grace and love help Jacob and his brother in this story too. They weep for joy at seeing each other, compare notes on how life has treated them, and agree to amicably go their separate ways. Jacob, whose hip has been injured in his all-night wrestling bout, goes away from the encounter a changed man. Even his name has changed, for God told him at the end of the night that he would now be known as 'Israel, because you have struggled with God and with humans and have overcome' (Gen. 32:28). I'm glad that my name doesn't change every time I get into a scrape with God or with people – or nobody would ever keep track of me ever again! That said, most of my hardest walks, like that one to the coffee shop, have brought me back changed in some way.

Is there a conversation, or an encounter, which you have been dreading? Have you put it off again and again, getting ever more creative in your reasons for doing so? Deep in your heart, you know that delaying it will do nothing to make it any easier. Isn't it time you tackled it?

Prayer

Dear God, I have rehearsed this conversation so many times in my head that it doesn't even sound convincing to me anymore. Please, please help me to find the courage to have it today. Like Jacob, I pray that I might find the courage to go through with it, and to come out better for it. Amen.

Walk 11

Joseph Walks into a Trap

> So Joseph went after his brothers and found them near Dothan. But they saw him in the distance, and before he reached them, they plotted to kill him.
>
> *Gen. 37:17–18*

The hall of residence where I spent my first year at university would never have won any prizes for beauty, I think. It was very utilitarian, and gathered all the residential blocks in a 'wheel' around the central hub, which held the offices and refectory. A fellow resident once told me that it was based on the design of a secure mental hospital in Sweden. I don't know. What I do know is that each landing in each block was identical, with four identical doors. On one occasion, three of the residents of such a landing decided to play a prank on the fourth. Day after day, they carefully taped newspaper over the outside of his doorframe. As was their intention, he got so used to this, that in the end he simply burst through the paper as if it weren't there. This blasé approach was the one they were looking for, which meant that on the last day they placed an open wardrobe behind the newspaper, he walked straight into it and they shut the door! Familiarity breeds contempt, as they say.

Joseph had allowed himself to settle into a very unhealthy pattern with his brothers. So convinced was he of his own present and future superiority, that he would speak of it rather too often. His brothers could not possibly pose any threat to him, since they were so far beneath him. How wrong he was! When Joseph's father sent him off to visit his brothers as they moved with the flocks, he was oblivious to the danger. First he walked to Shechem, only to discover they were not there. Next, he went on down the road to Dothan, and they saw him coming in the distance.

There is an almost exquisite irony in this, to which we as readers are privy. Joseph was anticipating a family reunion, but his brothers were anticipating revenge. He sees one thing, they see another and we yet another.

Had it ever struck you that God's view of us is like ours of the characters in this story? He can see what is coming. He can see both the innocent smile on Joseph's face and the ugly looks on those of his brothers. He can see the innocent spring in the step of the one and the furtive intent in those of the other. Our every walk, like the ones discussed in all the pages of this book, are observed, by God, from a distance. Wherever we go – up onto the mountaintops or down into the valleys where the sunlight scarcely penetrates, God sees us. He numbers the hairs of our head (Luke 12:7) as Jesus tells us, and probably counts our footsteps too.

Before you walk anywhere today, be sure of this – that God sees your path. He sees you as you crest the mountain and he sees you as you clamber down into the shadowy valley. And in all that, don't forget that he has plans for you. Joseph's innocent walk may well have led him into a trap, but his story was far from over. Ahead lay a famine, a season in jail, a rescue and a royal throne. This was just the beginning!

Prayer

> Dear God, I thank you today that my way is seen by you. Today I may think I am walking to a mountaintop, but in fact I may be heading for the valley. Wherever it may be, I know that you go with me, and I am glad. Amen.

Walk 12

Joseph's Brothers Walk into the Throne Room

'Come close to me.'... he said, 'I am your brother Joseph, the one you sold into Egypt! And now, do not be distressed and do not be angry with yourselves...'

Gen. 45:4–5

It was one of those moments when the phrase 'sick to my stomach' really rang true. For the past six weeks I had been overshadowed by what might best be described as a 'poison letter' with multiple signatories. They had met together to discuss their various dissatisfactions with me, and then put pen to paper in no uncertain terms. Now I was to hold a face-to-face meeting with all who had signed the letter, with one of the church leaders sitting by my side. It cannot have been more than fifty steps from my office door to the room where we were due to meet, but it felt like a very long way. It felt like a moment of reckoning, of a sort.

Such a moment was coming for Joseph's brothers. The annoying kid brother whom they had sold into slavery was now an official in the royal household of Egypt. After a trumped-up charge of theft, he now held their lives, quite literally, in his hands. With the doors locked and all his staff banished, he revealed his true identity to his brothers, weeping so loudly that his household could hear it beyond the closed doors. As his brothers looked on at this astonishing spectacle and realised what was happening, Joseph invited them to walk up to the throne.

I wonder if they exchanged panicked looks from one to the other as to who would go first? Did the eldest take the lead and walk up to throne before the others? Each step must have been measured out with a combination of hope and incredulity. Could this really be Joseph? Thankfully, they overcame their fears, stepped up close and heard one of the most remarkable explanations of sovereignty to be found anywhere in the Old Testament. Joseph explained that it was not them who had brought him to Egypt at all, but rather God who 'sent me ahead' (Gen. 45:5). His words rang with a grace and acceptance, which I still find astonishing every time I read them. The brothers' few steps up to the throne took them from a place of fear to a place of faith. They took them from the shadows of self-recrimination into the bright place of God's mercy. Thank goodness.

Sometimes the walk of fear is the walk of faith. I can remember someone telling me the tale of when he came to faith at a 'tent crusade'. Responding to a call to come up to the front and give his life to Christ, he was so frightened that he could not let go of his chair, and brought it up to the front with him! Thankfully, he learned to let go of it in the end, and has gone on to do great things.

Today, if you walk in fear, take a deep breath and try to walk in faith too. Those few steps into the unknown may just take you into a place of blessing.

Prayer

Dear God, like those brothers in the throne room, I feel almost rooted to the spot right now. Whatever will happen if I take these steps? Help me to trust you, I pray. Amen.

Walk 13

Balaam's Ass

When the donkey saw the angel of the L ORD standing in the road with a drawn sword in his hand, it turned off the road into a field. Balaam beat it to get it back on the road.

Num. 22:23

If I had ever met him, I think I would have been a little afraid of Martin Luther. His sharp mind and his ready wit would have made him a force to be reckoned with in any conversation. He could run rings around his detractors, and often did. One of his most witty responses was when the church authorities demanded to know whether he really believed that God was speaking through him, Martin Luther. He replied that it was easily possible and was reputed to have confirmed it by saying that 'God once spoke through the mouth of an ass'.[5] I would love to have seen their faces when he said it.

Our story today is the one to which Martin Luther was referring. Balaam was a prophet of God, and keen to be his spokesman. However, when this story occurs, he was still vacillating between being an entirely independent mouthpiece of God and being a prophetic voice for hire. He would get better in time, but at this point he was uncertain. As he headed off to declare his first prophetic message, God sent an angel to intercept him. Balaam did not even notice him, but his ass was more perceptive. Seeing the angel, we read that it 'turned off the road into a field'. This would happen twice more, with the ass pressing itself into a wall to avoid the angel, and finally lying down on the road with Balaam still mounted on its back. When Balaam threatened to beat it for its disobedience, God enabled it to speak and rebuke Balaam for his behaviour. At that point, the prophet finally saw the angel, and listened to him.

You may feel that such a story is out of place in our book of walks. After all, we are talking about walking on two feet, not trotting on four. That is true, but it is also true that the ass in this story is the one who shows the most faith and the most respect for God. It is the ass who spots the angel, not once, but three times. It is the ass who refuses to proceed when the angel is calling a halt. In terms of the spiritual journey, I am ashamed to say that there are many occasions when that ass has been much more perceptive than me. So many times in my life God has been stood in my path, or calling in my ear, and I have quite simply failed to notice him.

While it is not a good thing to dwell on our mistakes, it can be a good thing to review them once in a while. As you walk today, I wonder whether you could bear to look back at some of those moments when you have 'done a Balaam' – carrying on with your head down on a track of your own choosing, while all the while God was trying to get your attention? I'm sure you noticed in the end, but I wonder how long it took? Sometimes sitting with these mistakes in our mind can help us to avoid them in the future. Of course, it is possible that God might use a talking animal to set you straight as you walk. It is probably best not to count on it, though.

Prayer

Dear God, please will you forgive me for those times when an ass shows more spiritual perception than I do? Today, I ask for clarity and humility as we walk and talk. Amen.

Walk 14

Jochebed's Triumph

Pharaoh's daughter said to her, 'Take this baby and nurse him for me, and I will pay you.' So the woman took the baby and nursed him.

Exod. 2:9

I could not believe it, I really couldn't. The description of 'walking on air' sounds horribly clichéd, but it certainly came close. I was walking through the streets towards Paddington station after a remarkable meal in a pizza restaurant, and I could not have been happier. Four years earlier, I had written a little children's Christmas story – and had it locally published through a remarkable collaborative effort in aid of a local children's hospice. Now I had concluded a lunch with a literary agent and a publishing executive who had agreed to publish it nationally, and internationally. Had this really happened, I wondered?

Tucked away near the beginning of Exodus is the story of a remarkable mother, Jochebed. At the time she gave birth to her son, all Hebrew boys were under a death warrant from the Pharoah. Jochebed resolved to keep him hidden at home as long as she could, and after three months she came up with the scheme of hiding him in a basket in the river Nile. These days we would call such a thing a 'Moses basket' since that was the child concerned. When the day came to place the child in the river, his big sister was stationed to keep watch over him. Many of you will know the story. The pharaoh's daughter came by, decided to adopt the child, asked the girl hiding nearby to find a woman to care for him until he was weaned, and she fetched Moses' own mother. 'So', we read 'the woman took the baby home and nursed him.' By the time Jochebed walked home that day, her son was safe, his future was secure and she had royal gold in her pocket, paid to her for the privilege of raising her own son! I can just imagine the smile of knowing triumph on her face as she walked back to the house. God had been good.

I sometimes find I devote far more time to prayers of longing, or puzzling over the seemingly unanswered ones than I do giving thanks for the ones whose answers have come. It is as if the answer leads straight onto the next scheme or project, and I scarcely stop to draw breath, let alone to say thank you. It is a foolish thing, and it means that I miss out on a lot. I do hope that Jochebed paced out her walk back to the house with a thank you in every footstep.

Gratitude, like any other good habit, is one that we simply have to cultivate. Without stopping, intentionally, to give thanks once in a while we become like spoilt children, lapping up the good things and giving nothing in return.

Before you walk anywhere today, think about something for which you really ought to thank God. Consider it from every angle, like holding a gemstone up to the light. Turn it round and look at the different facets as they catch the light, acknowledging that each one deserves a thank you all of its own.

Prayer

Dear God, please let my footsteps today beat out a tattoo of gratitude to you. May I leave nothing out, but thank you with every footstep from beginning to end. Amen.

Walk 15

Moses Flees to Midian

When Pharaoh heard of this, he tried to kill Moses, but Moses fled from Pharaoh and went to live in Midian, where he sat down by a well.

Exod. 2:15

'Leave him.' These were the words of someone far wiser than me when I could see the person concerned walking away fuming with anger, regret and recrimination. I wanted to walk after them, to offer a listening ear, an arm round the shoulder, or maybe even a word of comfort. My advisor was quite right, though. At that moment none of those things would have helped. This angry person simply needed to walk out their anger, and maybe even to talk about it. What they did not need, at that moment, was me.

In the previous chapter we met Moses, the son of that ferociously protective mother, Jochebed. By her ingenuity and God's protection, he had survived the pharaoh's attempt to have every Hebrew boy killed at birth. Leaving his mother's house, he had grown up in the royal palace, wanting for nothing. One day, as an adult now, he went out to watch the Hebrew slaves working on some of Pharaoh's mighty construction projects. Seeing one of their Egyptian masters beating a fellow Hebrew, his blood boiled, he lashed out and he killed the man. Far from being grateful, the Hebrew slaves were resentful of the undue attention it brought to them, and wanted nothing to do with him. Moses, the rescued Hebrew boy with the charmed life, realised that his life was now in danger and fled to neighbouring Midian 'where he sat down by a well'.

What a different journey to Jochebed's, in the previous chapter. Here there was no triumph, only defeat. Resented by the Hebrews, outcast by the Egyptian pharaoh, Moses' feet took him to a land where he was a nobody. The journey may well have been more than 200 miles, and there would have been plenty of time along the way to regret his choices. Why had he not gone on living in the palace where he was well cared for? Why did he not remonstrate with the slave master, rather than killing him? Why could his fellow Hebrew slaves have not applauded his intent, rather than resenting his intervention? A wise man would certainly have told God all about these things along the way.

While I am not advocating a 'pilgrimage of gloom', there is a place in our lives for examining our regrets in depth, rather than belittling them or dismissing them altogether. David gives us a fine example of this in the Psalms, especially the psalms of lament, where he gives full vent to his sorrows, regrets and occasionally, his anger. Sometimes we need a long walk to ensure that a thing is forgiven and forgotten, rather than a short one which claims that to be the case.

If you have deep regrets today, then it might be a good day to take them for a walk with God. Put them in your mental rucksack right now – stuffed right up to the top, before you leave the door. God has all the time in the world for you to unpack them as you walk.

Prayer

> Dear God, today I pray for all your children who will walk angrily with you. They may be angry with themselves, their friends or even with you. Thank you for your promise to walk with them matching step for step, even if they are unaware of it. Amen.

Walk 16

Moses and the Burning Bush

I will go over and see this strange sight – why the bush does not burn up.

Exod. 3:3

A couple of days ago, I was talking to a friend who is part way through his training as a firefighter. He seems to love it. He loves the physical challenge, he loves the camaraderie, he loves the adrenalin, and he loves the noisy toys! Most of that I can understand. However, when he said, with a twinkle in his eye, that all his training was about running *into* danger rather than away from it, I realised how different we were.

When we reach today's story, Moses is living in exile. He has lashed out and killed an Egyptian slave master, thereby forfeiting his former privileges at the royal place. In fact, he has had to flee the country for the sake of his life. As the story begins, Moses is out in the wilderness, minding his own business and minding his father-in-law's flocks. All of a sudden, something entirely unprecedented happens. A bush bursts into flame, but is not consumed by the fire, which is freakish in every way. At this point, I would have stepped back a few paces, trying to work out what was going on, and distancing myself from the danger of sparks and flame. Not Moses, who walked over to the bush instead.

His curiosity paid off, because God spoke to him from the bush, thereby making him the first person to hear God's voice for many, many generations.

It is Moses' spiritual curiosity which would lead to his call, his commissioning and ultimately to the escape of an entire nation from slavery. It all started with him seeing the burning bush and feeling that he simply *had* to know more. Far from curiosity 'killing the cat' as the proverb goes, in this case it confirmed the suitability of the cat in question for the task ahead. Moses *had* to be the kind of person who *had* to know.

I sometimes think we are not as curious as we ought to be. The explorers of former generations had an insatiable curiosity to know what was over the sea or behind the mountain or at the other end of the world. Over the generations, and with the gradual expansion of knowledge we have lost that. Furthermore, that lack of curiosity sometimes seeps into our spirituality. We allow ourselves to be content with what we already know of God and the goodness of his which we have already tasted. We settle with that, and look no further.

As you walk today, ask God to use the things which you are seeing and hearing to stimulate your spiritual curiosity. What does that bird flying so high make you think about the heights to which you could ascend in your experience of God? What does that old, twisted tree make you think about the impact of times and seasons on your knowledge of your Maker? Try it, and see how your walk might be transformed.

Prayer

Dear God, please forgive me for a dull spiritual imagination which is too seldom stimulated by your Word and your presence. Today, I ask that you would call out to me, as you did to curious Moses from that burning bush.

Walk 17

Moses Goes Up the Mountain

The LORD descended to the top of Mount Sinai and called Moses to the top of the mountain. So Moses went up . . .

Exod. 19:20

I was preparing to preach on the subject of 'awe' and feeling that in fact I knew very little about it. Not only that, but I felt that the subject was little understood by those with whom I served, either. Understandings of the word were as varied as the people who held them. After discussing the matter with some tech-savvy friends, I came up with an interactive web page with a map of the world. People could drop a 'pin' anywhere on the map to indicate where and how they had experienced awe. The results were certainly illuminating. Just over half the respondents said that they had experienced awe in settings of natural beauty. Almost a quarter said they had experienced awe from their encounters with other human beings, and just under another quarter had experienced it in churches.

By the time we reach our passage today, Moses had faced down the Pharaoh, led an escape across the Red Sea, overseen the provision of manna from heaven and brought the people to the foot of Mount Sinai. Once there, a perimeter was set around the foot of the mountain, which no man nor woman was permitted to cross. After three days, thunder and lightning rolled around and around the mountaintop, terrifying those encamped at its foot. On the third day, God himself came down to the top of the mountain and called Moses to join him. The book of Exodus tells us quite simply 'So Moses went up'.

How terrifying a journey that must have been. Moses did not even have ignorance on his side. From the day of his first encounter with God in the burning bush, he had received ample evidence of the terrifying power which God held at his fingertips. He had seen him rain down plagues from heaven, split oceans, destroy armies and bring water from a rock. Moses knew full well who he was going to meet in the dark thunder clouds and lightning at the top of that mountain, yet still he went. If it were me, I think my footsteps would have grown slower and slower the closer I got to the top. No man had ever been invited to approach God like this before, so no one could tell him what to expect.

While I would never want to go through the experiences which Moses endured, I do wish that I had a greater sense of awe at the presence of God. I sometimes fear that the easy familiarity with which I talk to him in prayer has made me forget that I am, after all, addressing the architect of the universe. If I don't tremble when I pray, then perhaps I need to pray differently, or pray again.

As you walk and talk to God today, ask him to help you understand what it is to fear him without being afraid of him. If the vibration of each footstep as it travels up through your body could be a reminder of his holy presence, that would be a good thing, don't you think?

Prayer

> Dear God, I love to talk to you, and I'm glad that I don't have to be afraid of doing so. Remind me today, I pray, that to do so is an awe-inspiring privilege, and that I should not forget it. Amen.

Walk 18

Moses Walks Down the Mountain

His anger burned and he threw the tablets out of his hands, breaking them to pieces at the foot of the mountain.

Exod. 32:19

What would your definition be of disappointment, I wonder? Alternatively, what might be a defining moment of disappointment be, when your hopes or expectations came crashing down? One of mine came early on in my marriage. We had not long moved into our new home, and a small bedroom in the back of the house was to become my first-ever office. It had a desk and a table, but I needed somewhere to put my growing collection of theological books. Having them on the wall would help me to feel like a 'proper' minister, I was sure. It seemed to take me all afternoon to measure up the wall, mark the holes, insert the rawl plugs and fix the brackets. My wife had wisely stayed downstairs, out of the way, where she could not witness my ineptitude with all things practical. When there was an almighty crash towards the end of the afternoon, she called up the stairs lightly to enquire whether it was the books or the shelves which had fallen down. A small and very defeated voice replied that it had been 'both', and I headed downstairs with a look of abject and predictable defeat on my face.

I feel for Moses in our story today. He has been through so much already, including the sadness of exile, the fear of meeting God in the burning bush, the challenge of facing down the pharaoh, the dangers of the Red Sea crossing and the pleas for God's provision. Now, he has been rewarded with a face-to-face meeting with God on the mountaintop, but all is not well. Warned by God that the people are rebelling, he walks down the mountain with a growing sense of disappointment and anger. As he draws near to them, he sees the sight of them worshipping a golden calf instead of the God who has saved them, and it is all too much.

In that moment, the only example ever of God's own handwriting is shattered on the ground at his feet. Moses picks his way through the shards of the tablets with anger and dismay.

Have you ever done that? Have you ever found yourself picking your way through the wreckage of something which once seemed filled with promise and now reeks only of failure? The hopes which you had once entertained now seem like folly, and your heart is sore and bitter. We have all been there, in some shape or form.

For Moses it is not the end, because God will not allow it to be so. He is given precise instructions on what to do next and how to put this right, and before too long he is back on top of the mountain with two fresh stone tablets in his hands.

If you need to tread through the shards of that shattered dream again today, then by all means do so. Be sure of this, though – God does not give up. He did not give up on Project Moses, and he will not give up on Project You either.

Prayer

Dear God, it is hard to look at these shattered pieces and not feel that all is lost. Please reassure me that there is a good and onward plan, I pray. Amen.

Walk 19

Hur and Aaron Step Up

So Joshua overcame the Amalekite army . . .

Exod. 17:13

'Do you want a hand?' You have no idea how welcome those words were. I was training for RideLondon, a 100-mile cycle ride, and was halfway through one of my training rides. This one was about forty miles long, and I was on the homeward leg. I was somewhere between tired and exhausted, and the last thing I needed was the puncture I had just discovered. Not only that, but it was in my rear wheel, which meant removing the wheel, successfully negotiating the chain and gears, and then reassembling the whole thing safely enough to get me home. I was staring at the wheel in dismay when another cyclist appeared out of nowhere and offered to help me. If I knew his name, I would write to him this very minute!

Moses and the people of God had crossed the Jordan into the Promised Land, and there were many battles ahead. On this particular occasion, a vicious battle was raging in the valley outside Rephidim, with Joshua in command of the Israelite troops on the ground. Moses went up onto a hill to observe what was happening below, his faithful lieutenants Aaron and Hur by his side. He must have been grateful for their company at such a time. Every time Moses held his staff aloft, things went Joshua's way, but every time his arms grew tired and he dropped it down, the battle turned the other way. This was when Aaron and Hur had their 'fellow cyclist' moment. Instead of just watching, they stepped up, held Moses' hands for him until the sun went down, and the battle was won. Those few steps, from onlooker to helper, made all the difference.

There is plenty about Aaron in Scripture, but this is Hur's only moment in the spotlight, and thank goodness he was there. Being there with Moses in his hour of need was one thing, but stepping up and offering to do a thankless and uncomfortable task in order to help was quite another.

Over the years of ministry, I have lost count of all the Hurs I have met – unsung heroes who took the few steps to my side needed to sustain me in the battle. Sometimes their steps took them to the post box to send me a letter or card which assured me I was not alone. Sometimes their steps brought them close enough to place an arm around my shoulder, or occasionally to my front door with a homemade cake. On at least one occasion, it brought them up my drive with a jar of marmalade – a small gesture which said that the little things matter. I am unspeakably grateful for them all.

There is a very strong possibility that you could be such a person today. Your few steps could take you from onlooker to helper in such a way that a losing battle might get won. Go on, I dare you.

Prayer

> Dear God, thank you for all the Hurs in my life. Help me to be one for somebody else today, I pray. Amen.

Walk 20

Rahab Walks Up to the Roof

'Our lives for your lives!' the men assured her.

Josh. 2:14

Has it ever struck you how narrow the line is between triumph and disaster, or between safety and calamity? Sometimes it can be something as small as choosing *this* seat on the plane rather than *that* one, or turning down the first road rather than the second. A tiny decision, like a short walk, truly can make all the difference.

Our story today concerns a city with hundreds of houses in it. In those houses are hundreds of people making hundreds of journeys – some turning left and others turning right; some going upstairs and others coming down them. In this particular house are two spies, sent by Joshua to spy out the supposedly impregnable city of Jericho before he lays siege to it. The rumour is out that they are in the city, and they have been seen in the house of Rahab the prostitute. There are only moments to go before guards come to hammer on the door and take them away. This is the moment when Rahab makes her key decision and takes her short walk. She leads the men up the stairs to her flat roof and has them lie down beneath the stalks of flax which are drying there. In this way their lives are saved, and she strikes a bargain with them that she should be spared when the city falls to Joshua.

The men are as good as their word, and on the day the city falls, Rahab and all the family which she has gathered under her roof are spared. Not only this, but she ends up taking a place in the ancestry of King David, and thereby of Jesus. That is a big result for such a small walk.

Most of us have a natural inclination to believe that our actions are of little consequence. We think of them as tiny stones thrown into the vast pool of the whole world and causing only the very smallest of ripples. Rahab would tell us to see them differently, I think. Your decision to walk to *this* friend rather than *that* one today could make all the difference. Your decision to walk *this* way rather than *that* way round to the shops could mean that you bump into somebody whom you really need to meet. If one short walk up the stairs could save a whole family, imagine what your walk could do! And in all this, you and I have a ready access to God in prayer of which Rahab could scarcely have dreamed. We have every opportunity to dedicate our footsteps to him today before we take a single one of them.

Think right now about where you are likely to walk today – either near or far. Ask God that your simple walk might have consequences for good which you could never have imagined. I have no doubt that he will hear your prayer.

Prayer

> Dear God, today I give my every footstep to you. Please let today's journey take me to a place where you need me to be, I pray. Amen.

Walk 21

Joshua Walks Across the Riverbed

Yet as soon as the priests who carried the ark reached the Jordan and their feet touched the water's edge, the water from upstream stopped flowing.

Josh. 3:15–16a

I like to think I am generally up for an adventure, and to be honest I was on one already. It was four days since we had flown into Kathmandu airport, and had spent that time adjusting to the hustle and bustle of a city unlike any other. Now we were in Besisahar in Nepal's middle hills, and it was different again. To one side was lush jungle climbing up a steep slope, and to the other were the beginnings of the Himalayas. On this particular morning, the schedule allowed for a walk in the surrounding countryside. We left the little town below, and began to make our way along a country path to the river. When we reached the gorge, there it was – icy blue, glacial waters gushing down through the valley many metres below us. The only way to cross it was a narrow rope bridge, one person wide, which swayed as we set foot on it. At this point, my spirit of adventure began to quail a little.

Our story today takes place at the river Jordan, and I often wonder how Joshua was feeling by the time he got there. After the death of Moses, he had been thrust into the limelight and everyone looked to him for a lead. For three days now, the people had been camped on the banks of the river, which was rushing by at its flood height. The only way to gain the Promised Land was to cross it, and that seemed impossible. God, however, had other ideas. Everybody packed up ready to move, the priests lifted the heavy Ark of the Covenant onto their shoulders, and set foot in the gushing water.

It was, of course, just the miracle they needed, and everyone crossed over without getting a single foot wet. Spare a thought, though, for the priest to put the first foot into those gushing waters while balancing a gold-covered box full of stone tablets on his shoulder! All the tales of all the miracles in the past, including the crossing of the Red Sea, cannot have compensated for the terror of that moment. That irreversible walk of faith began with a single, and very public, step.

There will come a time for every Christian believer when the next obstacle simply cannot be crossed without a step of daring faith. To take that step may seem to defy all the odds. On the other hand, not to take it means staying *this* side of the land of promise, rather than enjoying *that* side. To step out may be frightening, but missing out is even worse. It is significant that the Ark of the Covenant was not carried alone. It had a pole thrust through rings on either side, and one priest stood at each end of each pole. There were four of them taking these courageous steps into the surging river *together*.

If you need to take a brave step of faith today, you may feel that you need to take it alone. After all, no one else can live your life for you. That said, try to make sure that you have others who can bear the burden of this step alongside you. This may mean praying for you, or talking with you on this side *and* the other of that step. While you are the one taking the step, they can still support you as you take it.

Prayer

Dear God, I know that like those priests of old I need to stop looking at this barrier in front of me and start crossing it. Like them, I feel that others are watching me as I do so. Please give me all the courage I need to get on and take the step today, I pray. Amen.

Walk 22

The Trumpeters Walk the Walls

 March round the city once with all the armed men. Do this for six days. Have seven priests carry trumpets of rams' horns in front of the ark. On the seventh day, march around the city seven times, with the priests blowing the trumpets.

Josh. 6:3–4

I am writing this now from my little office in North Wales. When I bought the house, the garden had two tiers, and the top tier at the back was a useless piece of waste ground overrun by brambles. A team of skilful craftsmen set about clearing the land and have built this lovely office on it. From its high position, there are views straight out to sea, and I can watch the wind turbines gently turning in Liverpool Bay. Of course, with any high view there is a drawback – the steps! For the first few weeks, the twenty or so steps up to the office were all part of the novelty. As winter set in, and the rain came lashing down, the novelty started to wear off. My office often doubles as a recording studio for radio and audiobooks, and I have discovered that I dare not do either of those things immediately after mounting the steps. Novelty is all very well, but no one wants to listen to a breathless voice.

I think the novelty must have soon worn off for the people in our story today too. The first time that Joshua and his army circled the city of Jericho with their trumpeters at the head of the line, it must have seemed quite a novelty. Even on the second and third days, they may still have smiled to themselves as they did it. I wonder how it felt on days four, five and six, though? If it bemused the people watching from the city walls, it must have done so even more with the soldiers and trumpeters themselves.

I suspect that it took far more effort to march on days five or six than it did on days two or three. Faith in the long haul can be far harder than faith in the moment. I look back to moments in my life as a church minister and recognise that sometimes God's call to stay and get on with it was harder than a call to up sticks and leave would have been. Simply carrying on and doing what you are doing until God calls you to do something else, can be the toughest call of all.

As a teenager, someone recommended the book *Steadfast Continuance in the Fulness of the Spirit*[6] to me. It was not the snappiest book title I have ever read, but then again it was not intended to be. As a teenager who wanted to change the world by teatime and rush onto the next thing, I needed to learn the value of sticking at it.

There are times in all our lives when God simply calls us to keep on doing the things we are doing. There is not much glamour or drama associated with them, and we are unable to see what their outcome might be. Like those trumpeters going round and round and round a total of thirteen times, we just have to persist. They are an example of persistence, and an object lesson in 'keeping on keeping on'. Could you do that for God today? If it feels like a tough ask, then tell him about it.

Prayer

Dear God, I know there is a value to this simple task which you have given me, but some days the repetition all gets a bit too much. There is a part of me deep down which just longs for a change. Help me to find contentment in what you have given me for today, and let you worry about what tomorrow might bring. Amen.

Walk 23

An Angel Walks into a Winepress

The angel of the LORD came and sat down under the oak in Ophrah that belonged to Joash the Abiezrite . . .

Judg. 6:11

How good are you at distinguishing footsteps, I wonder? In the house where I grew up, my bedroom was directly opposite the top of the stairs as they turned ninety degrees onto the landing. I always reckoned that I could tell exactly who was coming upstairs by the sound of their footsteps. Years later, when I had children of my own, I could do the same thing with the three of them. Each had a distinctive footfall. I wonder what sound might be made by an angel's feet?

In our story today, God's people are in a sorry state. Their disobedience to him had got them into all sorts of trouble, and now every time they planted crops, raiders would come across the border and steal them. It wasn't just the crops, either – sheep, cattle and donkeys were also being stolen. People were afraid. The fear is apparent when we meet Gideon, threshing wheat in a winepress. Threshing is usually done in the open air, so that the wind can carry away the unwanted chaff and leave the valuable kernel behind. Grapes, on the other hand, are crushed in a small and enclosed space. Gideon is threshing his wheat, or trying to, in a winepress. The writer of the story in Judges records, almost nonchalantly, that the angel of the Lord 'came and sat down' under a tree beside the winepress. As if his arrival weren't unnerving enough, he then referred to the preposterously occupied Gideon as a 'mighty warrior' (v. 12), which must have astonished him!

What I love about this story is the way that the angel simply walks up and sits down under a tree to interrupt Gideon as he works. There is no fanfare, no heavenly choir and no blaze of light, as far as we can tell. Sometimes the footsteps from heaven to earth are so soft as to be almost unnoticeable. Stories like this remind us that heaven really is close at hand, and that God is aware of exactly what is going on. He knew just where to find Gideon, even though it was an extremely unlikely place.

Of course, how that particular truth makes us *feel* on any given day is another matter entirely. I know that at those moments where I am thinking or doing something unworthy of God, I would be more than happy for him to be a long way away. Furthermore, I find the prospect of an angel slipping into step beside me all but unnoticed positively alarming. That yearning I feel for God's company on days of need has an equal and opposite pulling away on days of rebellion, I fear. Thank goodness he does not come at my beck and call, any more than the angel did with Gideon.

As you set out today, why not restate some truths to yourself as you put on your shoes and don a coat (if you need one)? Remind yourself that God sees your route before a single step of it is trod. Remind yourself, too, that it is he who chooses to walk alongside his children and not the other way round. Since he will be there anyway, why not welcome him, however you feel?

Prayer

> Dear God, I thank you that your commitment to accompany me is greater than mine to accompany you. I thank you that every promise you made to me when I started on this journey of faith is unbroken. As I step out now, let there be a gladness in my heart that you are there beside me. Amen.

Walk 24

Gideon Walks by Night

> Because he was afraid of . . . the townspeople, he did it at night rather than in the daytime.
>
> *Judg. 6:27*

On two separate occasions in my life, I have been inducted as the senior pastor of a church. It is a very public affair, with church members, visitors from churches and friends and family all in attendance. It is always an occasion of great rejoicing. On both occasions, I can remember walking, alone, into the empty church the following day and noting the contrast. Gone was the crowd and the noise, to be replaced with a quiet sense of the challenge ahead. This was the time to move on from commissioning to action.

We last met Gideon after a surprising encounter with an angel in a winepress. Things have moved on since then. The angel has confirmed his identity by making a rock burst into flames, and Gideon can be in no doubt that this is all deadly serious. Acting under angelic instruction, Gideon takes ten men with him and commits an act of courage and rebellion. He tears down the pagan altar outside his father's home, sacrifices one of his father's prize bulls upon it, and leaves a smoking ruin for his father and the neighbours to find in the morning. It was a seditious deed guaranteed to provoke an outrage. This was a flagrant challenge to the pagan god in whose name the altar had been erected. It is worth noting, though, that the whole thing was done under cover of darkness.

By the end of this chapter in Judges, Gideon will be demanding proofs of guidance with all the audacity of the great Patriarch Abraham. By the beginning of the next he will be reducing his army to a mere 300 on God's instructions and routing an enemy who outnumbered them many to one.

Within a few short verses he will have gone from a nobody to a soldier with a legendary military record for ferocity and courage. And yet, it all starts with him creeping around the village under cover of darkness with his ten friends!

I read this and I want to say, 'Thank God for small beginnings.' I thank God for Gideon's tentative steps in the dark before he took his bold ones in the light. In a similar way, I thank God for Daniel and his friends who would outlast empires, but who started it all with a protest over their palace dinners. (You can read the story in the book of Daniel, chapter 1.) Baby steps of faith, unseen by anyone but the person who makes them, are clearly visible to God.

The call on Gideon's life was a big ask. It would require faith and courage by the bucketload – but it all started with this walk by night. Is God calling on you right now to step out in faith? Maybe you can't quite do it in the full glare of the public eye right now – but you could maybe start in a hidden way. How about it? Take that thought with you, as scary as it may be, on your walk today.

Prayer

Dear God, I look at the later episodes in Gideon's life and I shudder. How could I ever aspire to a faith so bold or so public? Maybe today, though, I could take some tentative steps down the path you have shown to me. Help me, I pray. Amen.

Walk 25

Samson's Last Steps

Put me where I can feel the pillars which support the temple, so that I may lean against them.

Judg. 16:26

People often get remembered for their last words, but few get to choose the circumstances in which they utter them. I often encourage people, especially those who are terminally ill, to discuss with their partner how things will be at the end, and any wishes which they may have. The vast majority of people never get round to doing it, and often regret it as a result. From personal experience I can say that it is better to have a plan which you have discussed, even if it does not work out entirely the way you had intended. Planning for life's end, much as plans are laid for its beginning, is a good thing.

Samson's life had been full of sound and fury. He had been at different times a hero, a hooligan and even a poet of sorts. Now the end was coming. Blinded and bound, he had been in prison for some time when his captors were holding a party. In order to entertain their guests, along with a vast crowd of 3,000, they brought out the former strongman to do some tricks. This would be the moment when he would take his last few faltering steps. Speaking to the guard holding his hand, he asked him to guide him to a point in the temple where he could feel the pillars which held up the roof.

At that point, Samson asked God for one last bout of divine strength, that he might avenge those who had mistreated him so badly and trampled on the glory of God. The prayer was answered, the strength was given, and with one last almighty shove, the temple was brought down upon Samson and all those who were watching. It was an ending every bit as dramatic as the life he had lived.

Very few of us would ever want to make a name for ourselves as Samson did – with feats of great strength and brutality. However, the desire to make a mark, or to leave some kind of legacy so that we are remembered is perfectly natural. As a friend of mine occasionally says, we want to 'leave the world better than we found it'. We would like our last footsteps to lead us to a place where either we, or those we leave behind, can look back and say, 'That was a good journey.'

Where would you like your last steps to lead? Whereabouts would you like to walk between now and then? We don't always get to make the choice, but these are good and healthy questions to ask.

Prayer

> Dear God, wherever my steps may lead me before journey's end, I pray that I might bring glory to your name, and that I might leave behind the footprints which mark a good journey. Amen.

Walk 26

Ruth Walks to a Strange Land

> But Ruth replied, 'Don't urge me to leave you or to turn back from you. Where you go I will go, and where you stay I will stay. Your people will be my people and your God my God. Where you die I will die, and there I will be buried. May the LORD deal with me, be it ever so severely, if even death separates you and me.'
>
> *Ruth 1:16–17*

An old schoolfriend of mine used to describe me as someone who 'only opened his mouth in order to change feet'! In other words, he felt that I was often putting my foot in my mouth, usually by speaking before thinking. I am sorry to say that he was probably right! I have frequently found myself so keen to please or to impress that I make an offer before really considering whether I can follow through on it. It is a persistent character flaw, I fear.

In our story today, two young women, Ruth and Orpah, speak up with enormous courage. Both have been widowed and are without children. When their mother-in-law, Naomi, decides to return to her native land, they offer to go with her. This may sound like an obvious thing to do, but it would have been fraught with difficulties and danger. On crossing the border into Naomi's native Judah, they would have stood out a mile. Their accents would have betrayed them straight away. An initial entreaty from Naomi to think again falls on deaf ears, and they walk on together. A little further down the road she tries again, and this time their reactions are different. Orpah sees sense and turns back, but Ruth clings on, and in so doing utters one of the most beautiful descriptions of loyalty to be found anywhere in the Bible.

As open-ended commitments go, this one is without compare. This would affect not only the rest of Ruth's life, but the lives of all those who would follow on after her. By falling in step with Naomi, she enters into the family line which will one day lead all the way to Jesus. That said, I cannot read her story without feeling a certain melancholy for Orpah. Like Ruth, she started out doing the right thing. Like Ruth, she stepped up in a time of her own grieving to offer solace and companionship to another. The fact that she found herself unable to follow through with it makes her a familiar figure to many.

Have you found yourself rehearsing in your mind a promise which you have made, and feeling sick to your stomach that you are unable to follow it through? Do you feel something of a coward when you turn yourself around and go back the other way, instead of heading off in that new direction which had seemed so brave and so right before?

It is important to point out that as much as Ruth is honoured for her decision, there is no criticism of Orpah for hers. Not only that, but sometimes a journey may have many false starts before it really gets under way. Even then, it may head off in a direction other than the one initially intended. God knows your heart, and never takes his eye off you, no matter how many changes of direction you may feel obliged to make.

Prayer

> Dear God, this is one of those days when I want to be like Ruth, but I feel like Orpah. I feel like I have started off with such high hopes and ambitions, but they just don't seem to be working out. Please help me to set my eyes on you, rather than on the road for today. Let each footstep be a step of faith, I pray. Amen.

Walk 27

Ruth Walks in the Fields

Let me go to the fields and pick up the leftover grain . . .
Ruth 2:2

I became a Christian in my teens, and for some reason I had an idea in my head about a fixed hierarchy within the kingdom of God. To me, it was like an Olympic rostrum. At the top, in the slot usually occupied by the gold medallist, were missionaries. In my mind, these were brave people who gave up everything, and crossed oceans and borders to carry the word of Jesus with them. On the next step down, the silver one, were ministers and pastors. They had also given things up and thrown their lot publicly in with the cause of Christ. Even though the dangers were less obvious than those faced by the missionaries, they deserved a special place – a silver one. Then, on the bottom, bronze step, there were the rest of us, people like me.

Imagine my surprise and excitement, then, when I found myself 'promoted' to the top slot. I was to spend a year in cross-cultural evangelism, and I had the prayer letter and a commissioning service to prove it. With that last service at church behind me, I got the train, then the ferry, then another train to Brussels to get started. After a week of orientation, I transferred to a little town in the Ardennes. This was where the glamour and hardship of mission would really kick in, I was sure. In fact, the first week was spent redecorating the flat where the team and I were to live. The previous occupant had painted strident colours in gloss paint on the walls, and it all had to be sanded off before it could be replaced. Standing there with paint dust in my hair and a wire brush in my hand was not how I had envisaged life on the gold podium step at all!

In an earlier chapter, we encountered courageous Ruth, with her astounding open-ended pledge of loyalty to her mother-in-law. Her beautiful words spoke of a commitment to be there for Naomi through thick and thin, no matter what. Those words must have carried them through the long miles of the journey, and through the hostile stares and muttered comments as the they crossed the border back into Judah. With the journey over, though, the reality of their new lives became apparent. There was no one else to provide for them, so they had to provide for themselves. Seeing this, Ruth offered to go and find food. As she left their new home for the fields, I wonder how her footsteps felt? She had made such a brave and noble pledge of loyalty, but now it all came down to this – walking round a field with her head bowed, as she spotted the leftover bits of corn on the ground. It was hardly glamorous.

Often, though, God is more honoured in our ordinary moments than he is in our special ones, don't you think? Our brave and heartfelt commitment to him may be played out in stacking chairs or fetching a prescription from the chemist every bit as much as it might in preaching a sermon or crossing an ocean. Somewhere in the march of the kingdom, behind the brassy trumpets and the clashing cymbals, there is the soft padding of thousands of plodders, faithfully measuring out their calling in unsung footsteps. Ruth might well have seemed like one of them that morning, even though God had bigger plans.

Before you walk anywhere today, look at yourself in the mirror and say, 'My footsteps also count' – because they do.

Prayer

> Dear God, thank you for the example of Ruth, with her steadfast and unglamorous service. Make me content to walk the walk which you have allotted to me today, I pray. Amen.

Walk 28

Hannah Walks to the Temple

I am a woman who is deeply troubled . . . I have been praying here out of my great anguish and grief.

1 Sam. 1:15-16

Have you ever had a walk where you felt your legs literally could not carry you fast enough? Maybe you were on a mission to accomplish something, or quite simply late? I remember just such a walk over twenty years ago when I was working in a church to the south of London. I had been holding a conversation in my office with a person who was in real, desperate, urgent need. At the end of our conversation, I led him down the stairs to the building's exit, and closed the external door behind him. No sooner was he across the car park than I sped up the three flights of stairs to the office so fast that it was as if someone were pushing me from behind. I was not frightened nor pressured for time, but rather felt that I had not a second to waste before getting on my knees and praying for the person to whom I had been speaking. My feet were driven by a need outside of me.

In 1 Samuel 1, we find Hannah in a similar state of urgency. She had just sat through yet another awkward family meal. Yet again, she had been unable to disguise her bitterness and disappointment at being childless. As was usually the case, her rival had made no secret of her glee at Hannah's plight, and her husband had made a gauche attempt to comfort her. Excusing herself from the feasting table, she had pushed past the whiskery old priest at the temple's door and flung herself inside on God's mercy. Her prayers were too profound for spoken words, and the old priest simply saw her lips moving with no sound coming out. His accusation of her for being drunk brought a heartfelt description of her plight.

Can you imagine what it felt like to push past the sneering look of her rival, the anxious gaze of her husband and the critical eye of the old priest? That walk, from table to temple, must have felt agonisingly exposed and long. It was worth it, though. That heartfelt prayer brought her the son for whom she longed, and would bring to Israel a fearless priest and servant of God. One day it would be Samuel, Hannah's little boy, who would anoint David king.

Maybe there is a sense of urgency about your walk with God today. Right now, as you are reading this, you know that there is something troubling your mind and weighing heavily on your heart about which you simply have to talk to him. My best advice is to put this book down, right now, put your shoes on, and get out there to talk to God about it straight away. Let's pray, and then you can be on your way.

Prayer

Dear God, like Hannah of old, this need weighs heavily upon me. I can neither dodge it nor distract myself from it anymore. I am coming to talk to you about it, and I'm so glad that you are listening before I even say a thing. Amen.

Walk 29

Hannah Walks Back to the Temple

> Each year his mother made him a little robe and took it to him when she went up with her husband to offer the annual sacrifice.
>
> *1 Sam. 2:19*

It is one thing to make a hard journey once, but what about making it time and time again? During the early part of writing this book, I was settling into a new life in North Wales. It had so much to offer – including rolling seas and snowy mountains. However, there was a storm cloud gathering. Two hundred and fifty miles away, in south-east England, my mum was growing weaker by the day. As the frequency of my trips back across the border increased, so did my anxiety. Each trip there brought a sense of dread that I might have left it too late, and each trip back brought an equal sense of dread that I might have left too early. Those miles were elastic – stretched taut like a rubber band and ready to snap.

Think, for a moment of Hannah. When we last met her, she was pouring out her heart to the Lord with her great longing to bear a child. Her prayers were answered, she fell pregnant, and she made a vow that the child thus conceived would be given over to God in residential service at the temple as soon as he was old enough. Now, here is Hannah once again, making an annual trip to the temple to see her little boy.

I wonder how she must have felt on those journeys? Can you imagine the lightness in her step as she made the journey there – wondering how different he might look and how he might have grown in the intervening year? Bundled up somewhere in her baggage was a robe, bigger each passing year, as a mother's gift to her son. The journey home must have been much harder each time, each step taking her further and further away from her little boy for another year. Perhaps she took the previous year's robe back with her, held close as a reminder of the one she was missing? I know some people who turn old baby clothes into a patchwork blanket – like a reminder of all the years gone by. Perhaps she did that.

How often Hannah's obedience must have been tested in those journeys up and down to the temple. It was one thing to say that the child would be given over to the temple, but another to follow through on that promise, year after year. Sometimes the toughest kind of obedience of all is the repeated kind – where we must tread the same path of obedience again and again and again. Like the single act of daring obedience, it takes a degree of trust, but of a different kind. This is more of a marathon-style trust than a sprint, stretched out over the long haul.

You maybe find yourself on just such a path of obedience today. It could be many years since God called upon you to show your trust in him by taking on a particular role, or by turning down a particular opportunity. At first it was exciting, or even exhilarating. Deep down, there was the thrill that you, yes you, were stepping out in the kind of obedience that you associate with other Christians. As weeks have turned into months, and months turned into years, it feels very different, though. This marathon feels a whole lot longer and harder than you ever expected.

Prayer

> Dear God, like Hannah I want to obey you and go on doing so. I want to keep on this path until you tell me to turn off it. Can I just say, though, how hard it is? My feet are sore and my heart aches – so please give me your strength for this journey today. Amen.

Walk 30

Samuel Walks into the Temple

> The LORD was with Samuel as he grew up, and he let none of Samuel's words fall to the ground.
>
> *1 Sam. 3:19*

When I first started training as a Baptist minister, I had to spend one night a week away at college. I had young family at home and being apart was hard. Those thirty-six hours at college each week were precious, and I knew I should not waste a single one of them. When I wasn't in lectures, I felt that the rest of my time should be spent in the library – working on the assignments which would be so hard to squeeze in once I got back to the demands of church the next day. This being so, distractions were not welcome. On this particular occasion, I was working on an assignment in the library, when a voice came into my head again and again saying that I should go to the chapel and pray. At first I tried to dismiss it. When that didn't work, I tried to reason that since praying could be done anywhere, I could just as easily pray in the library. But the voice kept coming that I should go to the chapel and pray. With a sigh, I left my books open on the table, pushed back my chair, and made my way to the chapel.

In this chapter, we encounter Samuel, the little boy for whom Hannah had prayed so hard, and whom she had visited every year in the temple. At this point, he was working as a junior server to the priest, Eli, and learning the ropes. Each night, he would bed down in the temple itself, not far from the Ark of the Covenant. One night, as he slept, God himself came and called him. Not recognising the voice, Samuel walked into the room where the old priest was sleeping and asked what he wanted. Eli said it wasn't him, and sent the boy back to bed. A second time it happened, and a second time Samuel was sent packing. On the third occasion, Eli realised what was happening, and told Samuel to reply to the voice with the words, 'Speak, for your servant is listening' (1 Sam. 3:10). God went on to tell him terrible things about the fate that would befall Eli and his sons, and then the boy tried to go back to sleep. In the morning, the old priest summoned him with a dire warning that he should not hold back on sharing a single word of what he had been told, no matter how bad it might be.

Think of little Samuel, maybe with his knees knocking, making his way to Eli as the first rays of the morning sun fell through the temple. He must have felt sick to his stomach with the burden of the things he had been told. Would Eli beat him or scold him, or would he accept this dire judgement which had been entrusted to the little boy? How heavy his footsteps must have been on that morning as he made his way to deliver God's verdict. In the end, it did him no harm though, since we are told that: 'The LORD was with Samuel as he grew up'.

Meanwhile, back in the chapel at college, I sat and listened to another trainee minister playing the piano as I prayed. In the end, I went up to speak to him, and it turned out that he was wrestling with a horribly complex pastoral situation in his church, and needed someone to talk to. To this day, I am convinced that I was summoned to the chapel specifically in order to have that conversation. The walk from library to chapel took me no more than two minutes, but it took me all the way to the place where I was needed most.

Prayer

Dear God, like little Samuel, I am often afraid when you summon me. Like him, I am torn between being scared that I heard you wrong, and equally afraid of the consequences if I heard you right! Please, restore my trust in your goodness and your promises today, I pray. Amen.

Walk 31

Samuel Walks to an Anointing

> How can I go? If Saul hears about it, he will kill me.
>
> *1 Sam. 16:2*

How did it come to this? A couple of years before, I had walked into a charity shop and put my name down to participate in a 100km cycle race in order to raise funds for them. Now I was 'in the gate' with another hundred or so riders at London's Olympic Park. Ahead of me this time lay a 100-mile circuit through London, out to the Surrey Hills, and back again. I had dropped off my bag of kit, done a live radio interview, checked all my equipment, and now we were on a countdown from ten to the start. What a long way from a casual visit to a charity shop! One thing had very definitely led to another.

The last time we met Samuel, he was a young boy walking bravely from one part of the temple to another. Now his walk is quite different. Now he is walking into direct conflict with the king. With King Saul on the throne, the anointing of any other king was an act of sedition, and yet Samuel was about to do it. The more familiar part of the story comes a little later, when God tells Samuel that he looks upon the heart rather than the outside (v. 7). Before that can happen, though, Samuel must tough it out and make his way to Bethlehem, where a man called Jesse has eight sons to his name. There must have been real fear in Samuel's heart as he set out on his journey. So, he takes a deep breath, does as he is told and makes his way to Bethlehem, where eventually David will be anointed as king.

How close that came to not happening. If Samuel's fears had won the day, David would never have been anointed and the royal line which stretched down through the generations all the way to Jesus would never have begun. A thread of history which would change the world could not begin without a brave man, a bottle of anointing oil and a set of stoic but fearful footsteps.

Christians often struggle with knowing what it is that God requires of them. However, the greater struggles are often when they *do* know – because then they must get on and do them. I can remember the moments when God called me to serve overseas, the moment when he called me into pastoral ministry, and the moment when he called me out of it many years later. Each would require that I put one fearful footstep in front of the other and tell the people most directly affected by my decision what would happen next. On occasions, my feet felt like they were wearing old-fashioned diver's boots lined with lead weights. Nonetheless, that particular path had to be trodden.

Prayer

Dear God, I would love to tell you today that I am puzzled about your will for me. The thing is, I am not. I know what it is, and I know where I must go. Give me courage to walk my path, as Samuel did his of old, I pray. Amen.

Walk 32

David Walks into Battle

> David . . . with his sling in his hand, approached the Philistine.
> *1 Sam. 17:39–40*

It is probably one of those moments in my life when I have felt most exposed. Conducting weddings always made me nervous as a minister, and this one was no exception. On this occasion, though, it was a little different. The bride's family were stuck in traffic a long way away, and the ceremony was already late getting under way. I had offered the bride the opportunity to delay things by another hour, but she was adamant that things should go ahead. Her limousine went once more around the block, and then glided to a halt at the kerbside. As she was climbing out, an usher beckoned me towards him saying, 'Her mother is on the phone; you need to tell her that the ceremony is going ahead without her.' If this had been a movie, my footsteps would have gone into slow motion at that point, and my face would have shown the fear which was going on inside. Whatever would she say?

In our story today, young David has been wrestling with his fear. First of all, he must overcome his fear at telling the fighting men that they should be fighting and not hiding. After that, he must summon all his courage to tell the king that he is willing to fight the giant, Goliath, on his own. He must take another deep breath when he tells the king that he cannot wear the armour he has kindly provided. On leaving the king's presence, he heads to a nearby stream, selects five smooth stones, puts them in his bag, and heads off to face the giant.

There is a world of courage wrapped up in those words from the Bible passage. Behind David stood the Israelite army, alongside his sceptical brothers and the nonplussed king. Ahead of him stood a giant who had held the army in his thrall for days on end. What was a boy with his sling to do against a giant with his great sword?

Of course, we all know how the story ends, but if we look back a little further we can see how it started too. It started way before the giant or the battlefield or the king, when the shepherd boy David had learned to rely on God's help in tackling lions or bears that had threatened his flock. By the time he walked out with his five stones and his sling, he had already affirmed to the king and to anyone else who would listen that God would protect him. In fact, so convinced was he of this that eventually his walk broke into a run as he charged towards the giant and brought him down.

Whenever we take great steps for God, it is because we know that he has taken great steps for us. When stepping out in faith, we tread on the fulfilled promises which he has already lain down in our path. We know that he will provide because he has provided, and we know that he can answer prayers because he has answered them.

On your walk today, try to recall an answered prayer with every footstep. No matter how far you walk, you are likely to reach the end feeling better for it!

Prayer

Dear God, please forgive the spiritual amnesia which makes me so readily forget all the wonderful things that you have done. Today, I ask that you help me to remember some of them with every footstep. Amen.

Walk 33

Elijah Walks Away from God

Strengthened by that food, he travelled forty days and forty nights until he reached Horeb . . .

1 Kgs 19:8

Have you ever felt like you just *have* to walk away? I usually think that I am pretty good at maintaining a conversation, no matter how hard the subject. On this occasion, though, words quite simply failed me. What was supposed to be a dispassionate analysis of services in the church over a monumentally busy Christmas had turned instead into a festival of criticism. In the end, I did something which I have never done as a chair in any meeting, either before or since. I called time on the discussion, inserted a coffee break into the agenda, and went outside 'for some air'. Outside on that cold winter's night, I gulped down great lungfuls of the frosty air, and uttered some pretty heartfelt prayers, before I felt strong enough to go back in and resume the meeting.

Elijah had had enough. His life had consisted of confrontation after confrontation. After the latest of these – a very public showdown with the prophets of Baal, things got even worse. Queen Jezebel issued a decree for his immediate execution and he fled the scene. Initially he ran for more than a hundred miles, which was no mean feat in itself. Not surprisingly, on getting there he tucked himself into the shade of a broom bush and fell asleep. Twice an angel woke him from sleep in order to feed him. After the second meal he set off again, no longer running now.

What a strange walk that must have been. We are told that the journey took forty days, so there would have been plenty of time to think. On arrival, when God spoke to him, he was just as depressed and disillusioned as he had been at the start of his journey. If the intention of the walk was to 'work things out' then it had failed. Elijah was a prophet bent on ending his ministry, and even his final, dramatic encounter with God did not change that. After this, Elijah would anoint new kings to rule in Aram and Israel, and then proceed to anoint his successor. His forty-day walk had been his last hurrah, and he would not stride the prophetic stage again.

Talking to God about endings can be every bit as important as asking him about beginnings. Ministries, or tasks, or roles which start well need to end well too. If you know that some particular chapter of your life is coming towards its end, then you should maybe take a long walk and tell God all about it. You can talk about the things you will miss and the things you will be glad to lose. You can look back on highs and remember the lows. There is no need to walk for forty days, like Elijah, and you can always split it over several walks!

Prayer

> Dear God, I think this particular chapter is reaching its end for me. It has been so good, and I have been so grateful for the privilege. Now that the end is in sight, help me to reach it with dignity and strength, giving glory to you, I pray. Amen.

Walk 34

Elijah Walks to Heaven

> As they were walking along and talking together, suddenly a chariot of fire and horses of fire appeared and separated the two of them, and Elijah went up to heaven in a whirlwind. Elisha saw this and cried out, 'My father! My father! The chariots and horsemen of Israel!' And Elisha saw him no more. Then he took hold of his garment and tore it in two. Elisha then picked up Elijah's cloak that had fallen from him and went back and stood on the bank of the Jordan.
>
> *2 Kgs 2:11–13*

Despite not having an athletic bone in my body, I have always loved the film *Chariots of Fire*. In part, this is because of its depiction of principled Christian values; and in part because much of it was filmed in St Andrews, which is a very special place to me. The Carlton Hotel, featured in the film, was in fact my hall of residence for one year. Despite all of that, it took me many years to discover where the phrase 'chariots of fire' came from.

Before our passage today, the prophet Elijah and his sidekick, Elisha, have been on one of those awkward walks where you both know it is going to end before too long. It must have been a bit like walking round the airport terminal with a best friend, knowing that very soon their flight will be called and they will be whisked away. The end of an era is at hand.

Elisha must have felt bereft. It was all very well knowing that this moment would come, but it cannot have made it any easier. Upon his shoulders, now, lay the prophetic mantle for a people who would not always listen. Even if he had inherited the 'double portion' of Elijah's spirit, for which he asked (2 Kgs 2:9), the burden imposed upon him was enormous. Elijah's last walk had been an easy one – a few steps from the ground and into the chariot, which then spirited him away to heaven. Elisha's would be a harder one – back across the Jordan to a land of doubt and disbelief.

When he struck the waters with his master's cloak, did he really believe that they would part, I wonder? We shall never know. Either way, the waters obediently retreated to right and left, leaving him to make his first prophetic walk alone with dry feet. Steps of faith are always big steps, no matter how far we are going.

Standing on the banks of the Jordan there can have been no doubt in Elisha's mind about where he should go. There may have been all kinds of hesitation, but he knew clearly where the path should take him next. We all have to make that kind of walk once in a while; a walk where we know exactly what is needed even if we can scarcely face it. If you have one ahead of you right now, maybe even one which you have been putting off again and again, now would be the time to tell God about it.

Prayer

Dear God, I really envy Elijah in this story – whisked away from all his troubles on a fiery chariot to heaven. How easy that would be! Instead, I stand here like Elisha, clinging onto his master's old coat and hoping for the best. Please help me to take whatever steps I need to today, I pray. Amen.

Walk 35

A Man Walks to the Door

> When the servant of the man of God got up and went out early the next morning, an army with horses and chariots had surrounded the city.
>
> *2 Sam. 6:15*

When was the last time you breathed a sigh of relief so heartfelt that it was audible? There is a nature reserve near me, and I often like to walk there with the dog. There is a winding path up through the shady forest, past an old, ruined manor house, and out onto the chalky summit where there are views up and down the coast for miles. On this particular occasion, I had parked in the car park, instead of on the road, as I usually do. Starting from this different location, I had a cursory glance at the map and information board and took the nearest path. This proved to be a bad move. The path was unfamiliar, and within half an hour I was spectacularly lost. I tried again and again to find my way out, either up or down, without success. Finally, I met a fellow walker, who saw my rather frazzled expression, and directed me to the main pathway, with strict instructions not to deviate from it until I saw somewhere familiar. When I finally did, almost an hour and a half after my walk had begun, I breathed a sigh of relief.

In today's story, Elisha the prophet and his servant are in trouble. They have angered the king of Aram, and during the night he has sent his army to surround them. When morning comes, we read that the prophet's servant 'got up and went out' only to be confronted by the terrifying sight of the army bent on their capture. This is where the miracle comes, and the moment where that man's early morning walk got transformed. Elisha prayed that his eyes would be opened, and beyond the king's army he suddenly saw God's army, arrayed across the hillside in chariots of fire. The relief must have been palpable. Needless to say, Elisha and his servant escaped unharmed. I wonder whether that man's first walk out of the front door every morning was ever the same again?

It is important to note that the miracle here is not God *sending* the army, but rather the servant *seeing* them. The hosts of God were already there to protect his servants, it's just that they had not seen them before. Presumably they had been there all through Elisha's previous adventures and encounters with those who opposed him. There they were, ready to march at heaven's bidding, even when they could not be seen.

Stories like this make me wonder quite how spiritually unobservant I am. Do I go through each day unaware of how close heaven's armies may be? Do I walk through each day's journey, unaware of the angels with whom I rub shoulders, and the business of heaven, which God is transacting all the time? If I do, then I am sure I am not the only one.

As you get ready for a walk today, why not ask that God would part the curtain just a little to afford you a glimpse of the greater things going on around you? To be honest, it is probably best if he does not show you a sky full of chariots of fire, especially while crossing a busy road! If you could come back from your walk just a little more aware of his hand at work, though, wouldn't that be something?

Prayer

> Dear God, I thank you for this story, and for those magnificent chariots of fire to assure your servants that all was well. As I walk today, please give me the tiniest glimpse of how you are at work, I pray. Amen.

Walk 36

Naaman Walks to the River

So he went down and dipped himself in the Jordan seven times...

2 Kgs 5:14

Believe it or not, one of the hardest aspects of my job as a minister was wedding rehearsals on the night before a wedding. Now, weddings are supposed to be glorious, happy occasions, of course. Rehearsals, however, can be a different matter. All the participants are nervous and excited, and often it is the first time they have seen their bridesmaids or best man since the invitations went out. There is so much nervous energy in the room, that often the last thing they want to do is to listen to the minister and concentrate on the task in hand. Often, the thing which takes the greatest amount of practise is the walk of the bride down the aisle. Once they have got it cracked, though, they walk down the aisle with as much poise as if they were queen for the day, which is probably how they feel.

I imagine that the character in our story today had a lot of poise. Naaman was the commander of the national army of Aram, and in good favour with the king. On telling the king that he needed help with his leprosy, and that there was rumoured to be a prophet in Israel who could help him, he was dispatched immediately with the king's blessing and a letter for the king of Israel. That king was unable to help, and in the end Naaman beat a path to the door of Elisha the prophet. Elisha did not come to the door but sent a message to say that the great soldier should wash seven times in the Jordan and then all would be well. Affronted that the prophet would not even meet him in person, Naaman stormed off into the distance. It was only when his servants calmed him down that they persuaded him to try the prophet's cure. They pointed out that if the task had been a difficult one, Naaman would have done it straight away. Instead, the simplicity of the request irked him. In the end, their persuasion succeeded, and he entered the river.

What a different figure he must have cut to his usual poise and swagger. Here was the great general, with men at his beck and call, stripped down and walking reluctantly and alone to the bank of the river. I imagine that his shoulders were a little stooped and his head slightly bowed, very unlike his usual military bearing. Naaman is not so very different to the rest of us, in that we might embrace a dramatic calling from God, but struggle to accept an ordinary one. If we are going to put ourselves out in his service, we deem, it might as well be in some dramatic or admirable way. Where is the glamour in doing the ordinary thing? The truth is that the wheels of the kingdom of God would grind to a halt tomorrow were there not tens of thousands of Christian men and women doing ordinary things with extraordinary humility for the sake of the king. They do them at God's command, much as Naaman eventually bathed in the river at the prophet's command.

Today's walk might be a good time to bring the sheer ordinariness of your life to God. You could maybe talk about the humdrum things that will fill your day, but ask that you might do them at God's command and for his purposes.

Prayer

Dear God, sometimes I would love to do the heroic thing for you, striding out into the world to do great things and win public victories for you. Today is not that day, though. Today I will try to honour you in the ordinary things, and pray with all my heart that you might make use of them. Amen.

Walk 37

Four Lepers Take a Midnight Walk

> So they went and called out to the city gatekeepers and told them, 'We went into the Aramean camp and no one was there – not a sound of anyone – only tethered horses and donkeys, and the tents left just as they were.'
>
> *2 Kgs 7:10*

Have you ever been a collector of stamps or postcards or beer-bottle caps or anything else? For many years I have been a collector of regimental military badges. It all started with a couple bought with my pocket money on a nearby market stall, and the collection now numbers more than 350. I have sought them out in junk shops and antique fairs and all sorts of other places. Sometimes it can be a bit too consuming, though! There was a town we used to visit occasionally whose streets were positively packed with just the right kind of shops. Sometimes, I would be aware of my pulse quickening a little as I parked the car, excited by the prospect of all the treasure I might find. To admit that does not put me in the best of lights, but it is true to say that my heart really would beat faster as I headed down the high street into those wonderful shops.

The characters in our story today are not seen in an entirely positive light, either. God's people have been under siege from the Arameans, and those within the city walls are starving to death. The four lepers in this story are not allowed inside the city on account of their disease and must fend for themselves. Under cover of darkness, they head for the enemy camp to see if they can forage any scraps of food. In fact, the camp is deserted, and they begin to gorge themselves on the food they find, and then begin looting all the gold and silver they can lay their hands on. Part way through the night, they realise that what they are doing is wrong. To enjoy all this plunder while others within the city were fading away was not right, and would surely get them into trouble. 'So', we read, 'they went and called out to the city gatekeepers and told them'. The gatekeepers told the palace officials, the palace officials told the king, and the king sent charioteers to verify the story.

How did they feel as they picked their way out of the camp and headed for the city gates, I wonder? Were they overwhelmed with a sense of guilt, or still enjoying a certain smug delight that they, the outcasts, had got there first? Maybe it was a mixture of the two.

In truth, so much of our service to God arises from mixed motives. We are rarely capable of true selflessness, but instead serve him with the kind of muddled hearts which reflect our flawed humanity. Even footsteps taken in the kingdom's cause may be footsteps which combine courage with fear and generosity with selfishness.

Perhaps it is time for a very deep breath before you take your walk today. Honesty is rarely uncomfortable with God, since you are not telling him anything he does not already know. It is literally impossible for you to shock him. Why not take a moment to look back at those moments of service which others have hailed as selfless but which you feel were not? Like the walk of the lepers to the city gates, other people benefited from those moments no matter what, and that is a cause for rejoicing.

Prayer

> Dear God, you know that I have not always served you from a pure heart, no matter how it may appear to others. Today, I just want to be honest with you about that, and to see what comes next. Amen.

Walk 38

Nehemiah Walks into the Throne Room

I prayed to the God of heaven, and I answered the king . . .
Neh. 2:4–5

This was not my first visit to Serbia. By this stage, I had been on numerous occasions to teach in a local Bible school, and I was starting to get the hang of it. I knew what was where, I was a little more familiar with the food, and I had got into the rhythm of teaching through a translator, stopping after each phrase. This particular afternoon was a break from the classroom, since my students and I were joining a group of visitors in order to distribute aid to nearby refugees. There would be a small gathering in the local community hall, after which the aid would be distributed. As the coach pulled away, the man in charge of the event leant over the back of the coach seat in front and said, 'You are preaching when we get there.' The next fifteen minutes were spent in the back of the coach huddled with one of my students, as we worked out what I might say and how he might translate it!

Nehemiah was a long way from home, a Jew in exile. He had found himself with a job in the winter palace of the emperor Artaxerxes, and was making the best of his situation. The arrival of news from Jerusalem broke his heart, though. The very idea that the city and its temple were in ruins affected him so deeply that he spent many days in fasting and prayer. After that, he returned to work, but his was a nervous walk as he approached the imperial throne with the emperor's cup of wine. His face gave him away, and the emperor asked him whatever was the matter. How dare he tell him, when it was the emperor's troops who had wrought so much of the havoc that was breaking his heart? Taking a deep breath, he told him the whole sad tale, and must have been taken aback when the great Artaxerxes asked him what it was he wanted. We are told that 'I prayed to the God of heaven, and I answered the king'.

Those few steps towards the throne, and the brief prayer which accompanied them, would change the future for Nehemiah and for all his countrymen. It may have been short, but it was a real walk of faith. Many of the walks in this book are long ones, as people pace and pray out a knotty problem with God. Sometimes, though, we need to do the same thing in double-quick time. We may need to fill the few paces from waiting room to consulting room with a prayer. Equally, it may be the few paces which takes us from a reception area into an interview room for a new job which need to be turned into the lines of a prayer for help.

Clearly it worked wonders for Nehemiah, as he ended up getting free passage back to Jerusalem, all the timber he needed, and a royal guarantee of safe conduct all the way. My quick prayer in the back of the bus worked too, and I ended up preaching the gospel in that Serbian community hall in front of a giant statue of Lenin, which was something of a novelty.

Prayer

> Dear God, it might not be today, but please help me to remember that one day, when the crisis comes and I feel I scarcely have time to think, I do have time to pray. Amen.

Walk 39

Nehemiah Paces the Walls

I went up the valley by night, examining the wall.

Neh. 2:15

I have often been told that I have the very opposite of a poker face. In other words, I find it exceptionally hard to disguise what is going on inside of me at any given time. If I am happy, or sad, or burdened or itching to tell people about something, it will be very obvious. Sometimes as a church leader it was my undoing. In my desire for openness and my excitement about the possibilities of an idea forming in my head, I would often share it before it was wise to do so. The result was that the idea – and frequently the person responsible for it – fell flat on its face.

Nehemiah has done the unthinkable, and asked the emperor Artaxerxes for permission to visit the ruined city of Jerusalem. With royal permission and protection, he has made the journey, and arrived with enough wood to get the project underway. If this were me, I would have called a public meeting, and said to the poor wretches living in the rubble: 'Guess what, it's all going to be fine and God has granted me his favour.' That is very much *not* the approach which Nehemiah took. On arrival in the city, he stayed there for three whole days without taking any discernible action. On the night of the fourth day, he snuck out of the city all alone to make an inspection of the damage under cover of darkness. Where some gateways were impassable, he picked his way along the outside wall instead.

Only after this did he go public and summon the people at large to help him. This was astute leadership on his part. The people left in the ruins of the city were defeated, frightened and surrounded by hostile neighbours.

If he was going to raise their hopes of rebuilding the city upwards from the rubble, he had to be sure that he fully understood the enormity of the task for himself. To address them before this night-time walk would have been both foolish and dangerous.

Maybe you have a good scheme in your mind. Maybe you are almost convinced that God has something in particular for you to do. It may be challenging and difficult, but you know that God is with you, so it is sure to work out. If you are simply bursting to share the idea, then why not take a leaf out of Nehemiah's book and take one more prayerful walk before you do so? If God is in it, you will come back from your walk more convinced than ever. If he is not, or at least not now – then you will have saved both yourself and others from some hurt.

Prayer

> Dear God, you know that I feel 99.5 per cent convinced that this is just the right thing to do. I want to let people know and then I want to get on with it. Help me to take a breath as I walk and talk with you today, though. Maybe that other .5 per cent will come . . . and maybe it won't, but I would rather know. Amen.

Walk 40

A Queen on a Mission

So Esther approached and touched the tip of the sceptre.

Esth. 5:2

I was talking to my friend, and it was not an easy conversation. Until earlier that week, he had been an elite athlete and an Olympian. Just a few days before, a persistent injury had finally got the better of him. In the very public setting of a major running event, he had pulled up and hobbled off the track. By walking off the track, he was walking out of high-level elite competition for good, and he knew it. They were just a few steps, but they changed everything.

Esther is one of the most unusual books in the Old Testament, since the name of God is never mentioned in its pages. However, his presence is there on every page. The eponymous Esther's cousin, Mordecai, gets wind of a plot to annihilate all the Jews in King Xerxes' kingdom. The roots of antisemitism run old and deep. Since Esther has been selected from all the king's harem to be queen, she must have some access to him. So Mordecai urges his relative to intercede with the king on the Jews' behalf. This was much more dangerous than it sounded, since to approach the king without a royal command was to attract a sentence of certain death. When the day comes, Esther loiters in the courtyard opening onto the throne room, hoping to be spotted. The king does indeed spot her and holds out his golden sceptre as a sign that she may approach.

What a long walk that must have been. Close your eyes, and you can almost hear the sound of her sandaled feet on the stone floor, the swish of her clothes and maybe the jangle of some jewellery. Every other voice is hushed and it is what some would call a 'tumbleweed moment'. What would happen to this courageous young woman, and would she survive? Amazingly, the king not only allows her to approach, but promises to give her whatever she requests, even if it should be half his kingdom. The things she does ask for will lead to a rescue of the Jews, the execution of their enemies, and a Jewish festival which is still celebrated to this day. Time stands still as this brave woman crosses the floor and risks her life.

Today might be a good day to remember those whose walk of faith places them in danger for their lives. On this very day, the decisions they make to walk tall for God may well cost them liberty or life itself. Why not ask God to help you keep them in mind as you walk? The last thing those brave Christian women and men would want is your pity, but they do need your prayers.

Prayer

Dear God, I thank you for Esther's bravery, and for her steps into harm's way on behalf of others. Today I pray for your strength for those women and men whose lives are under threat because of their loyalty to Jesus. Make them strong, and let them know that someone, somewhere is praying, I ask. Amen.

Walk 41

A Walk Back to Job

So now take seven bulls and seven rams and go to my servant Job and sacrifice a burnt offering for yourselves.

Job 42:8

I did not want to walk through that door. I had requested the meeting, put it in my diary, and arranged for somebody to accompany me. All the same, I did not want to go in. Behind that door was the author of what could best be described as a poison letter. Without going into the details of the letter, it had stated that the author no longer wished to be in the church if I were its minister, and that their preference would be for me to go. This was going to be an awkward encounter in every way imaginable, but also unavoidable.

The walk in our story today was also unavoidable. The three people walking it had been building up to this for a long time, without even knowing it. Eliphaz, Bildad and Zophar had spent the past weeks supposedly 'counselling' the godly man Job when his life started falling apart. In fact, there had been little wisdom and no comfort in any of their words. They had done nothing to make Job feel better, and had only heaped criticism on top of his many other woes. When at last God set Job straight, it was time for him to do the same with these three other men. They were told to collect what was necessary for a generous sacrifice, and 'go to my servant Job'. After that, they were told, he would offer the sacrifice, pray for them, and God would say no more about it.

That must have been a very sober walk to Job's house, don't you think? Did they argue with each other about who had said what and when, I wonder? Then again, after God's rebuke they may have felt too ashamed even to make eye contact with each other and walked the whole way with their heads bowed. Their words had done them few favours so far, so maybe they felt that silence was the better option. We have all known occasions when we feel that uttering a single extra word will only add to the trouble into which we have already got ourselves. Instead, we opt for an uneasy silence which seems to say it all.

Christians are sometimes perceived as those who are always wagging their fingers about other people's sins, but in general I have not found that to be true. In fact, I think we are rather more inclined to treat our sin too lightly than too severely. So accustomed are we to the limitless and wonderful grace of God that we airbrush out our sins as if they had never been, and carry on regardless. If we had been walking beside these three burdened men, I think we would have found their pace too slow and rushed onto something more interesting instead.

Once in a while, it is not a bad idea to take our sins with us on a walk with God. There is no need to exaggerate them, and definitely no need to invent them – since there are plenty of them without the need to make any up! All the same, to take the time and the rhythmic pace of a walk to talk to God about them again can be a healthy thing. He loves to listen, and occasionally we need to overcome our own reticence to talk.

Prayer

> Dear God, I know that there are many ways in which I have let you down. I ask you to help me remember some of them, not so that I can drown in sorrow, but so that I can shed them through confession and plunge joyfully into the clear water of your grace again. Amen.

Walk 42

A Walk Together

If either of them falls down, one can help the other up.
Eccl. 4:10

It was maybe not the most auspicious of beginnings for a lifetime's partnership, but my wife to be and I met at a 21st birthday party when all the good Christian students were away on a Christian Union house party. As the evening drew to a close, I offered to walk her home, and instantly regretted it. There was snow on the ground, my dress shoes had no grip, and my legs went from under me. As I lay sprawling on the pavement, though convulsed with laughter, she bent down to help me up. In truth we would spend the next thirty years and more helping each other up. When raising three children wore her out, I would help her up. When church life felt more like a Circus Maximus than a theatre of dreams, she would help me up. When cancer was making its relentless march through her body, there were times when she could walk only with me to help her up. When she fell for the last time, it would be God who helped her up, never to fall again.

It is maybe because that motif has been such a feature of my life that I wanted to include in this book the touching description in Ecclesiastes of two people walking together. There the writer explains that two are better than one, and goes on to say that: 'If either of them falls down, one can help the other up.' That has been true for me within the narrow confines of marriage, but true also within the wider context of Christian fellowship. A church is a group of people bound by a covenant to walk with each other, which may often necessitate catching the other when they stumble or fall.

As a Baptist for many years, this particular motif is very familiar to me. Baptist churches are gathered, covenanted communities, held together by a commitment to God and to each other. Some of them will renew a formal covenant each year, and these often include phrases about 'walking together' or 'watching over one another'. The latter is not intended in an intrusive or authoritarian way, but rather as a commitment to be there for each other whenever the going is tough. At times when I have fallen through physical or spiritual exhaustion, I have been unspeakably grateful for those who gave me a shoulder to lean on, or prayed for me until I could get to my feet again. In the very best sense, they have been my guardians.

Who has walked by your side on this journey of faith? Who has kept up with you when you were striding confidently, or slowed down for you when your burdens made you barely move? They may be spouses or friends, mentors or pastors, but whoever they are, they have done you a great service. Why not pick the name of one of them to carry with you on your walk today? It would be good to spend that walk composing a message of thanks to send to them on your return. It doesn't have to be elaborate and flowery, but it would be good if it were so specific to them that it could not possibly apply to anybody else. Take that name with you now and see what you have on your return.

Prayer

Dear God, I thank you for this special person, whose patience, strength, encouragement and prayer has sustained me on the hardest parts of my journey. When my message of thanks arrives with them, I pray that it might be fuel for their journey too. Amen.

Walk 43

Daniel's Friends Walk in the Furnace

Look, I see four men walking around in the fire, unbound and unharmed, and the fourth looks like a son of the gods.

Dan. 3:25

Have you ever been in the position of seeing a storm coming, even from a long way off? Living by the sea, and having a dog to walk, I really should get better at reading the signs. Many is the time that I have gone out underdressed and ill-equipped for the simple reason that I failed to take note of the inevitable storm on the horizon.

There was a sense in which the storm in today's story had been coming on the horizon. Daniel had been 'spoiling for a fight' for a long time. Right at the start of the book which bears his name, we learn that Daniel and his three fellow captives in the royal palace in Babylonia began a campaign of small but determined opposition to their captors. By refusing to eat the meat prepared for them in the palace, they demonstrated that they belonged to God, rather than to King Nebuchadnezzar, who had taken them captive. This kind of defiance was sure to lead to an almighty showdown before too long. Indeed, it was not too long in coming, and in chapter 3, Daniel's three friends are thrown into a furnace for their refusal to worship an idol erected by the king.

Unable to turn away from the spectacle, the king watches in horrible fascination as they are cast into the flames. As he looks, though, he sees something entirely unexpected, with four figures, rather than three.

While the effect on the king is immediate and dramatic, leading to the rescue of the men and an immediate declaration of allegiance to God, we hear nothing from the three men themselves. Shadrach, Meshach and

Abednego (to give them their Babylonian names) escape unscathed, but what of their walk through the flames? We know that their faith was strong and defiant before they went in, declaring their unwavering faith in God, whether they should live or die. What exactly did it feel like to walk round in the flames – like a walk in the park, with God to protect them? We shall never know, at least not from their lips.

That said, there are plenty of Christians who can tell you of their sense that God has walked through the flames with them. They can talk of their times in a hospital bed, or a prison cell, or boat adrift at sea, and their utter conviction that God was with them. He still walks in the flames with those who trust him.

Wherever you walk today, know for certain that he walks with you. You may not see him or hear him, but he is there; and we know this because he has promised to be with those who walk in his name.

Prayer

> Dear God, some days I find it so much easier to see the flames than I do to see you. However you choose to do it, let me know that you are there today, I pray. Amen.

Walk 44

Daniel Walks from the Lions' Den

 The king was overjoyed and gave orders to lift Daniel out of the den.

Dan. 6:23

Did you know that you can now find the word 'ta-da' in many English dictionaries? Definitions vary, but most centre around a dramatic entrance, or the announcement of something spectacular or surprising. It is a word I have taken great relish in using when calling on someone who is not expecting to see me because I live a long way away. Somehow, it just seems to add to the moment.

I would love to have been there at the moment when Daniel strode, unharmed, from the lions' den. After defying the king's commandment not to pray to anyone except the king himself, Daniel is charged with praying to God. As a valued advisor, the king tried many ways to save him from his fate, but no legal recourse was available. When sundown came, Daniel was consigned to his fate, and the lions' den sealed above him. With the first rays of the sun the next day, the king came anxiously to the den, maybe a little stooped with his great sorrow. To his delight, Daniel called out that his God had indeed saved him, and 'the king was overjoyed'.

I wonder how he emerged from the den towards the king? Was there a swagger of triumph or a spring in his step, I wonder? Whenever I read this story, I think of the thirty-three Chilean miners trapped underground for sixty-nine days in 2010.[7] When at last they were rescued, they stumbled out of the rescue capsule blinking in the glare of the arc lamps and smiling at their first breaths of surface air. A terrible fate had been reversed and a great rescue performed. They were free, and alive and oh, so grateful. I imagine Daniel must have known exactly how that felt.

Most of us are rather timid in displays of emotion when it comes to God. We are hesitant to express the depths of our sorrow or despair lest it seem ungrateful to him. Equally, we are hesitant to express the heights of our joy, lest something else were to befall us. These concerns are false, I think – and should no more be entertained than Daniel should have walked from the lions' den as if it were nothing at all. If God has done a good thing for us, then there is no reason why it should not be our feet as well as our hearts that skip to his tune.

As you walk today, why not take some time to dwell on a blessing which really makes you smile? It may be the moment when you first came to faith some years past, or the joy of a baby's smile a few minutes ago. Why not give vent to it right now, as you walk along? If someone wonders why you are smiling from ear to ear as you walk – you can always tell them!

Prayer

> Dear God, forgive me for my polite sorrow and my timid joy. Today, help me to feel those things about which I pray so deeply that they show on the outside, I pray. Amen.

Walk 45

Hosea Walks the Walk of Shame

So I bought her back for fifteen shekels of silver and about a homer and a lethek of barley.

Hos. 3:2

There used to be a TV quiz show where every contestant who was knocked out would have to 'walk the walk of shame'. It wasn't a walk of shame really. It was just a walkway with banks of flashing lights and a lot of exaggerated booing from the audience. A real walk of shame is something entirely different. A real walk of shame is when you feel that everybody knows your business and that there is nowhere to hide. You have probably walked it on occasions yourself.

Hosea paid a very high price for being a prophet. His life itself would become an illustration of the message about faithlessness and restoration which God wanted to convey to his people. As his ministry gets underway, God instructs him to marry a woman who will be unfaithful to him. He duly marries Gomer, and she bears two sons and a daughter. Sometime after that, she moves out of the family home and begins to live the life of a prostitute. However, the story is not over yet, and Hosea is told to go and bring her back.

What must that have been like, I wonder? To walk through the town, where everyone probably knew Gomer's reputation, laden down with a sack of barley, and then to walk back with her on his arm? Had net curtains been invented at the time, I have no doubt that they would have been twitching. By the time Hosea and Gomer got home to their children, the tale of Hosea's walk of shame was doubtless all around the town. For him the emotions of shame at what had been, relief to have Gomer home again and anxiety about what might happen next must have been inextricably mingled. Just what, exactly, was God up to this time? The times when God's will runs counter to our own inclinations and plans are the times when it is hardest to follow.

Although it is a Methodist tradition, I used the annual covenant service throughout my time as a Baptist minister. As close to the start of the year as we could, we would make a covenant to God and to each other. As I watch Hosea walking down the road, shoulders stooped beneath the burden he bears both without and within, I am reminded of these words from that service:

> Christ has many services to be done:
> some are easy, others are difficult;
> some bring honour, others bring reproach;
> some are suitable to our natural inclinations and material interests,
> others are contrary to both;
> in some we may please Christ and please ourselves;
> in others we cannot please Christ except by denying ourselves.[8]

To obey God by doing something which runs counter to both our gut instinct and our own rationale is a hard call indeed. And yet, sometimes the cause of God simply cannot advance without the courage of women and men of faith who will lay aside their own inclinations in order to follow his sovereign and puzzling will.

You may not be in such a position today, but the chances are that you will be at some point in your life. As you set out on your walk today, ask for a humble heart which is willing to accept God's will, no matter how unthinkable it might seem.

Prayer

Dear God, I thank you for Hosea's walk of faith, and I thank you for the hope that was made plain in both his words and his life. Today, I ask for a willing heart, that I might follow you no matter where you lead nor how you do it. Amen.

Walk 46

Jonah Walks Away

But Jonah ran away from the LORD and headed for Tarshish. He went down to Joppa, where he found a ship bound for that port.
Jonah 1:3

On my 21st birthday, my father presented me with a signet ring. It had been passed to him by his father, who in turn had received it from his. The seal, in bloodstone, bore a lion rampant holding a cross. Now, although such crests could easily be bought in the nineteenth century, placing it on my finger really made me feel like *I was somebody*. I had ancestors and a signet ring and everything. I suppose if I had been suddenly told of a fabulous inheritance, the feeling might have lasted a little longer.

The prophet Jonah was a nobody, or at least we know next to nothing about him. We are told that his father was Amittai, but we do not know anything about him, either. As far as we know, Jonah's life was unremarkable. That all changed on the day when God spoke to him out of a clear blue sky and commissioned him with a message for a distant city. To serve almighty God as a spokesman was the highest calling Jonah or any fellow Jew could ever have imagined. This was the kind of thing of which dreams were made, and insured a kind of immortality in all the generations to come. Jonah, however, did not see it that way. Rather than heading for Nineveh, where his mission lay, he walked off in the other direction.

What a sight he must have been, running away from home with the little that he could carry, and constantly looking back over his shoulder to the place where the dreaded commission had been given.

We all know that this journey will end up taking him to the hold of a ship, the bottom of the sea and the belly of a 'huge fish' (v. 17); but right now, it is looking almost risible.

The thing is, I do not believe there is a single Christian believer who has not 'done a Jonah' at some point. We may not have run away, but we have done our level best to avoid the call of God. We have dodged *that* question or studiously avoided *that* person or ingeniously made ourselves absent from *that* situation, all to avoid the one thing we know God requires of us. Repeated too often, such things become a habit.

Time for an honesty check on your walk today. As you step out through the door, resolve to review with God some of those moments when you have 'taken the Jonah option', avoiding the very thing that God wanted you to do. The aim is not to indulge in a guilt trip, but rather to clear away some of the rubbish that stands in the path between you and God. Do not leave it another day.

Prayer

> Dear God, you know and I know that there are plenty of moments when I have 'done a Jonah'. I might have hidden them well from others, but you see them all. In the honesty, let there be healing, I pray. And when the healing is done, let resolve come in its place. Amen.

Walk 47

Jonah Walks to a Sulking Spot

Jonah had gone out and sat down at a place east of the city.
Jonah 4:5

Are you good at sulking? I know I used to be. As a teenager I perfected the long-suffering sigh, followed by an eye roll and finished off with a perfectly timed stomp out of the room. I imagine that those towards whom I was directing my displeasure could not decide whether to sigh right back at me, or to laugh at how stupid I looked.

In our story today, the erstwhile runaway Jonah is back on track. He has survived a near drowning and an uncomfortable journey in the belly of a large fish. After that, he has done what God required him to do, and walked the length and breadth of the city of Nineveh, warning all its citizens that they face punishment from God unless they repent. With that job done, he has a sinking feeling in his heart. The feeling is born out of a fear that the people will repent, that God will forgive them, and that people whom he regards as unacceptable will end up folded in God's warm embrace. He just can't abide the prospect of it, and decides to find a vantage point where he can watch the whole ghastly thing unfold.

For a man who had been almost drowned, walked from the beach to the city, and spent three days on a preaching tour of that city, the effort to find his vantage point and then build a shelter on it must have been considerable. Those of us who know the pleasures of a good sulk probably feel it was worth it, though!

I talk as if it is funny, but sulking with God is no laughing matter. Whenever we do it, we shut ourselves off from the sunshine of his grace and deny ourselves the sweeping vista of his power at work in the wide world. To sulk at the deeper mercy and wider heart of God is to turn ourselves into sullen children who cannot enjoy what is best for us. I know, because I have been there. I suspect that many of you have too.

Before you walk anywhere today, take a long, hard look at Jonah as he makes his way out of the city. His brow is furrowed as if wrestling with a problem too big for him. His mouth is set in an unforgivingly straight line, and his head is bowed as if afraid of catching sight of God above by accident. Does he look at all familiar? If he does, then maybe a little repentance might not go amiss today.

Prayer

> Dear God, without too much effort on my part, I can easily look back and see these Jonah moments of mine. They have never made me happy, and I am fairly sure they have made you sad. Please help me to walk with you today as one who is truly glad to be yours, I pray. Amen.

Walk 48

The Magi Walk Away from Bethlehem

> Having been warned in a dream not to go back to Herod, they returned to their country by another route.
>
> *Matt. 2:12*

This was not how I had planned for things to go. There had been an application form, an international flight, a six-hour interview and further prayers and reflection. To minister in this international church in a buzzing city at the heart of Europe would have been so exciting. The prospect of preaching week by week in a church with translation booths at the back set my heart racing. And yet, and yet. At the very heart of all this was something which was not right for me, a piece of theology with which I could never be comfortable. In the end, I had to ring them up and walk away, tears flowing as I did so. Sometimes the obvious way is not the God way.

Matthew is the only gospel writer to record the journey of the Magi to visit Jesus. These exotic figures, maybe Zoroastrians from Persia, underline the global significance of the Christ child in the manger. On arrival in Jerusalem, they are summoned to the palace by King Herod. After an audience with him, they are released with an instruction to report back to him when they have found the child. To do so would have been courteous at least. Of course, we all know the story of how they travelled to Bethlehem, found the child, and presented their gifts. However, when they left, instead of turning one way and heading to the palace, they turned the other and headed back home.

To do this was to make themselves fugitives from a king whose short fuse and ill temper were legendary. He had various members of his own family executed merely on the basis that he thought they *might* have been plotting against him. Herod was a dangerous enemy.

Sometimes the steps which God calls on us to take are in entirely the opposite direction to the ones we would choose for ourselves. Common sense, instinct and prior experience may all point in one direction, and yet the way of faith lies in the other.

One of the greatest privileges of my life has been to help people discern their call to full-time pastoral ministry. They have come from all walks of life and at all different stages of their life. They have all shared two things in common, though: a strong conviction that this is the call of God, and an equally strong amazement that it should be so.

Today would be a good day to pray for those who are having their Magi-on-the-threshold-of-the-stable moment. A journey lies ahead of them, but right now they know that it is not in the direction which they would have anticipated. They may feel excited, anxious, or just a little overwhelmed. Maybe you could stop once or twice on your walk to pray for them. A crossroads or junction in the path would be a good place to do it.

Prayer

> Dear God, right now, I pray for those who have experienced a call from you to change the direction of their lives. I ask you to confirm that call in many ways and on many occasions, please. Amen.

Walk 49

Walking to Egypt

Get up . . . take the child and his mother and escape to Egypt.
Matt. 2:13

Have you ever walked in such a way that you felt that at any moment someone might 'rumble' you? A few years ago, I was flying to another country to visit a Christian charity. Over the years, they had discovered that the best way to get the money that lovely Christian people had raised for them was to have it brought out in cash. In consequence, I found myself in an international airport with a padded envelope containing many thousands of pounds in cash in my hand luggage. At my insistence, I also had a letter detailing what it was and for whom it was destined, just in case. I have never felt so uncomfortably aware of my hand-luggage in my life. Throughout my time in the airport, I did not let it out of my sight, no matter where I went.

In Matthew's Gospel, shortly after the departure of the Magi from Bethlehem, it is time for Mary and Joseph to be on their way. King Herod is in a dangerous mood, and the baby Jesus' life is in danger. An angel, possibly the same one who had visited him in a previous dream, appears to Joseph in the same way with the stark warning to head for Egypt.

Just as his distant ancestors had fled out of Egypt centuries before, so now Joseph flees into Egypt. Except that it is not the same way at all. They fled with the treasure which they had wrested from their Egyptian neighbours, but he fled with something infinitely more precious. In his arms and under his care was the precious little bundle of Jesus. His treasure, unlike the gold and jewellery of his forebears, was nothing less than the Messiah of God. As he and Mary made their way across the border into Egypt, they carried with them one promised by prophets and prayed for since generations past. What a responsibility!

On occasions, though, it is good to be aware of the enormity of the task that God is entrusting to us. Years ago, someone asked me on a Sunday morning if I ever got nervous when I preached. She smiled when I replied, 'Every Sunday.' I went on to explain that if ever I stopped feeling nervous, then that would be the day on which I stopped preaching. The sense of the gravity of what I was doing – speaking a God-word to those in all kinds of needs – weighed heavily upon me. I explained that this was a good thing, since the weighing heavily led to leaning heavily on God himself for inspiration, for strength and for insight. Like Joseph carrying his precious bundle, I would carry my precious sermon into the pulpit with me, trusting that God would take care both of it and of the people who listened to it.

What is the precious burden, or responsibility, which God has given you to carry today? Instead of leaving it at home when you walk, take it with you. Turn it over in your mind and heart as you pace through your journey. You may find yourself talking both positively about the responsibility and negatively about the burden, but that's OK. These things can be held in tension, and they often are.

Prayer

Dear God, as I walk today, I shall be thinking of Mary and Joseph, holding their precious burden close on their dangerous journey. I shall reflect on their sense of responsibility even as I reflect on my own. Since you gave me this thing, help me to carry it, I pray. Amen.

Walk 50

People Walk to the River

People went out to him from Jerusalem and all Judea and the whole region of the Jordan.

Matt. 3:5

I wonder whether you have heard of the 'Velvet Rope syndrome'? Reputedly it dates back to 1894 and the opening of the Waldorf hotel in New York City. When it opened, they placed a red velvet rope across the entrance to the lobby. This instantly had the effect of generating a curiosity about what might lie beyond the rope, and who might be permitted to cross it. Today, a 'velvet rope' marketing strategy is one that promotes the exclusivity of an event or experience in such a way as to make it more desirable. It is a variation on the theme that a crowd draws a crowd.

John the Baptist was not the first and would not be the last radical preacher to preach along the banks of the Jordan. He was probably not the first to claim inside knowledge on the arrival of the Messiah, either. Even so, this wild man with his camel-hair clothes and his foraged diet of locusts and honey drew quite a crowd. John writes that these people came not just as spectators but participants. They were confessing their sins and asking John to baptize them in the Jordan River.

How do we explain the magnetism of this odd character, John? Why were people walking out of the towns and cities and villages of the region to make their way to the riverbank? In order to answer that question, I need to take you to a football stadium in South Norwood, London, on a summer's evening many years ago. I was staying up the road at the time, at Spurgeon's College. I was there on a residential study course all about the theory and techniques of preaching. As a break from our studies, my fellow students and I had taken the evening off to attend a Billy Graham rally in the stadium. In truth, there was nothing spectacular about the preaching, and Dr Graham probably broke many of the rules that we had been taught that very week. It is not the preaching I remember. What will stay with me forever is the sound of creaking and banging as hundreds and hundreds of people left their seats and walked down to the front in response to the preaching. God had summoned those people, it is as simple as that. Like the crowds flocking to John at the riverbank, they were drawn by someone beyond themselves.

To be propelled by the Spirit of God towards a challenge or an adventure that you scarcely understand can be a thrilling thing. To find yourselves caught up in the Spirit's breath, like a boat with its sails full, skimming across the surface of the water, can be one of the most exhilarating experiences of human existence. Maybe today will prove to be one of those days when God seems to propel your footsteps in a particular direction and you are unsure what it may mean for you.

Prayer

Dear God, today I am really unsure where you are leading me. The only thing I *am* sure about is that you *are* leading. Help me to follow, knowing that I will understand when the time is right. Amen.

Walk 51

Jesus Walks Down to the Water

> Then Jesus came from Galilee to the Jordan to be baptised . . .
> *Matt. 3:13*

As we opened the doors of our air-conditioned taxi, I was struck by two things. The first was the dusty heat of an unclouded sun. The second was the hiss of airbrakes and the noisy burst of chatter as a group of tourists disgorged themselves from their coach. We were at the river Jordan. More to the point, we were at the car park for the 'original baptismal site' on the river Jordan. To one side was a gift shop, selling such trinkets as olive-wood carvings and small bottles of river Jordan water. To the other was a cinder-block toilet. Like the other tourists, we embarked on the snaking path down through the trees and bushes to the water's edge. For some, it was a moment of genuine pilgrimage, while for others it was simply a curiosity. All had travelled great distances to be there, though.

In Matthew's Gospel, the arrival of Jesus has been heralded with the most spectacular fanfare. He starts with the genealogy, setting Jesus in context against the backdrop of the whole of Jewish history. Then he tells the story of his birth and is the only writer to include the exotic Magi from the East. After that comes the escape to Egypt and the ministry of John the Baptist. Now the stage is set for his dramatic speaking part. And yet, his first act is simply to come, as many others have done before him, to the bank of the river Jordan and ask John to baptise him. There is something so understated about Matthew's description when this much anticipated and gloriously heralded Messiah arrives at the river.

How can it possibly be so ordinary? As Jesus himself goes on to explain, no drama is required, for this is a simple act of obedience and nothing more.

I love the way that stories like this ennoble the ordinary and invest it with spiritual significance. To the casual observer, there was nothing to set Jesus' baptism apart from all the many others which John had been performing. He was simply doing what was required. Of course, God would affirm in dramatic fashion that he approved of the act, by sending down his Spirit on him. Then again, doesn't he still do that when men and women of faith take ordinary steps and do ordinary things out of their extraordinary love for him? If God has called you to do something for him today, it doesn't matter how small or insignificant it might seem to the casual observer, to the one observing you from heaven it is precious and honourable. Doing it for him is what matters most.

As you put your shoes on to walk today, think about the most ordinary things you may do in his service. Think about the card of encouragement which you will walk to the post box to send. Think about the cake you will bake for a friend. Think about your visit to a worker at the church just to tell them that you are grateful for what they do. All these things may be as truly steps of faith as were those which took Jesus down a well-worn path to the water's edge at the Jordan. Obedience to God is a beautiful and powerful thing.

Prayer

> Dear God, I thank you that Jesus no more shied away from doing the ordinary thing than he did the courageous thing. Help me to do the ordinary with extraordinary faith today, I pray. Amen.

Walk 52

Jesus Walks into the Wilderness

Then Jesus was led by the Spirit into the wilderness . . .

Matt. 4:1

Have you ever felt inexorably drawn to a particular place at a particular time? The feeling can be so strong that it defies all logical explanation. If someone were to stop you on the way there and ask you why you were making the journey, or even if they were to ask you the same question when you actually got there, you might find yourself unable to answer. All you know is that you have to be in this place at this time.

Our story today comes right after the dramatic moment of Jesus' baptism. It is as if all the gospel up to this point were the overture, with the sound of the orchestra gradually getting louder. This, surely, is the moment when the anointed Messiah of God will step out onto the stage and perform some miracle so dramatic that it will convince everyone in an instant? In fact, Jesus does just the opposite. He walks away from the limelight, not into it. Not only that, but he does so at the specific urging of the Spirit.

It is the Spirit who leads Jesus away from all the opportunities of his new ministry and into a place where he will be tempted by the devil.

When I visited the Judean wilderness, I saw it through the tinted windows of an air-conditioned minibus, but even then, it was possible to tell what a harsh environment it is. Small scrub-like plants are few and far between, and the rocks are almost white, blasted by the sand into waveforms which reflect the sun back onto the road. It is not a place where I would wish to spend one whole day, let alone forty of them. How did it feel for Jesus to walk away from the familiarity of Galilee and the high point of his baptism into this unforgiving place? Of course, unlike us, it would have been many times worse for him because he would have *known* what to expect. For him, there was not only the isolation and deprivation, but the inexorable certainty of a clash with his enemy. To know that it was a clash that he would win does nothing to detract from the costs involved.

So often we think of Jesus' suffering as being entirely encapsulated in the cross. If we think of a walk of suffering with him, then it is the walk up to Calvary with Simon carrying his cross. The thing is, there were many footsteps of sorrow before that, and these, into the wilderness, must have been some of them. The cosy years in the family home in Nazareth were gone, and the glory days of miracles and astonished crowds were yet to come. These footsteps into the blistering heat of the wilderness and towards the enemy who awaited him there were already marking out the true cost of incarnation.

We naturally shy away from sorrow; it is a reflex reaction to do so. Today, though, why not ask God to let you in on the sorrow of Christ as he walked into the wilderness to face the devil? As you plant your footsteps one in front of the other, think of him doing the same, with each leading him closer to his terrible battle. He did it because he loves you.

Prayer

Dear God, it makes me unbearably sad to think of Jesus walking away from the lovely moment of his baptism and into this terrible place. Help me to carry it with me on my walk today, that I might know greater depths of his love for me. Amen.

Walk 53

Peter Walks on Water

> Then Peter got down out of the boat, walked on the water and came toward Jesus.
>
> *Matt. 14:29*

This trip had not gone well. My son was living for one year in the French Alps and wanted to share something of the experience with me. I thoroughly enjoyed the trip up into the mountains, as the coach passed through the clouds and came out in a sunny upland of brilliant white snow and cerulean blue skies. Even strapping on the skis for the first time was something of a novelty, but it turned out I had absolutely no flare nor appetite for skiing. After trying out the most basic techniques of all, we took a chairlift up to the top of one of the milder slopes. When we reached the top, and my struggle to release the bar across my knees resulted in an undignified fall into the snowdrift below, it did not auger well for what was to come. After picking myself up, I edged to the start of a slope that would take me onto the ski run proper and I froze with fear. I simply could not move. In the end, it was only when my son placed himself on the downward slope, assuring me that if I fell he would catch me, that I was able to make a tiny bit of progress. There was no escape from my fear without his presence and his voice.

By the time we reach today's story in the Gospel of Matthew, the disciple Peter has seen some amazing things. He has seen Jesus raise people from the dead and give others back their sight as well as feeding a crowd of thousands from one tiny picnic. In other words, he knows that Jesus can transcend the limits of possibility by his power. Maybe this is why his instinct when he saw Jesus walking on water was not to back away, but to believe his explanation that it truly was him and not a ghost. In fact, Peter went further than just believing, and wanted to be part of this historic miracle.

Asking Jesus to command him, he got out of his boat and took the first steps ever taken by an ordinary human being on the surface of water.

We tend to dwell on what happened next, when Peter lost his nerve, panicked, cried out and had to be plucked from the water.

Let's reflect for a moment, though, on those first few steps. In these days of 'step counts', we don't know whether there were ten or twenty or just a few of them. All the same, every single one represented a courage that no one had ever shown before. Maybe we should celebrate Peter for his bravery rather than shake our heads at his weakness. For those few seconds he was genuinely superhuman, in that he had transcended the limits of human nature.

If our walk of faith teaches us anything, it is that we can do more than we ever thought possible, with God's help. Even though our steps of faith may be few and our faith journey feels very short, nonetheless we can transcend all manner of limitations. Faith steps are always giant, no matter how much distance they cover.

Why not ask God to remind you on your walk of every step of faith which you *have* taken rather than those which you have missed? You might be pleasantly surprised!

Prayer

Dear God, what a figure of faith Peter cuts as he steps out of that boat to walk across the water towards you. Even if my faith feels weak today, please remind me of the days when it has been strong, I pray. Amen.

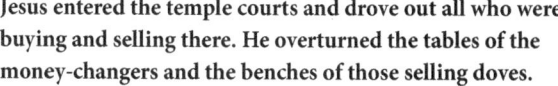

Jesus Walks into the Temple

Jesus entered the temple courts and drove out all who were buying and selling there. He overturned the tables of the money-changers and the benches of those selling doves.

Matt. 21:12

During my school years, I acted in many plays, and then continued that on into my first two years as an undergraduate. I loved everything about it, from the smell of the greasepaint to the hot glow of the lights and that nervous anticipation of listening out for your next cue line. That anticipation was never greater than the moment of waiting in the wings for your first entrance. This was the moment to make an impression. Sadly, on one occasion I made a spectacularly bad one. I was playing 'Ratty' in *Toad of Toad Hall*, and had a stiff tail attached to the back of the blazer I was wearing. As I strode onto the stage ready to utter my first line, the tail caught in Mole's papier-mâché molehill, turning it around and revealing both its chicken-wire construction and its startled occupant to the audience. While memorable, it was not the entrance for which I was hoping.

Read carefully, each of the four Gospels has a drumbeat in the background – getting louder and quicker as the time nears for Jesus to come to Jerusalem and fulfil his destiny. The writers leave us in no doubt that it will be dramatic and significant. I suspect, though, that none of them anticipated Jesus' entry into the temple courtyard. Matthew records that he 'entered the temple courts and drove out all who were buying and selling there'. In case we think that he simply asked them to leave, the picture is very vivid, as Matthew continues, 'He overturned the tables of the money-changers and the benches of those selling doves.' This would have been a scene of pandemonium, with coins rolling across the floor, angry tradesmen unseated from their benches, and maybe even accidentally freed doves flying away into the blue sky high above Jerusalem. Jesus was, without a doubt, 'making an entrance'.

Every time I read those words, I am struck by how narrow I have allowed my mental picture of Jesus to become. When I think of him, I see the baby in the manger, the healer bent over the sick, the teacher on the mountainside and the Saviour on the cross. I hardly ever see this angry figure, striding through the temple as if he owned the place (which he did). Again, I can close my eyes and imagine the sound of his voice as he gently asks a sick person, 'What do you want me to do for you?' (Mark 10:51), or his warm tones as he explains yet another parable privately to his disciples. At a pinch, I can even hear his last great cry of triumph from the cross. This angry voice in the temple, though; and the angry footsteps which carried him across it, are much harder to imagine. Mine is a tame Jesus, whom I have tamed unconsciously for my own benefit.

Would you dare to ask God to introduce you to this other Jesus as you walk today? Would you ask for some insight into the anger which exploded into action on that bright morning when he strode into the temple and upset everything from tables to expectations? Your prayer will surely be heard, and you might be surprised by the answer.

Prayer

> Dear God, these are footsteps of Jesus which I have pretty much ignored. I have been uncomfortable with them, and a little afraid, if I'm honest. Please help me to see them clearly today, and to understand what they tell me about him. Amen.

Walk 55

The Dead Walk

> The bodies of many holy people who had died were raised to life. They came out of the tombs after Jesus' resurrection and went into the holy city and appeared to many people.
> *Matt. 27:52-53*

What is the strangest thing you have ever encountered while out walking, I wonder? One of mine was when I lived near London's Bushy Park, and encountered a man playing his bagpipes to a herd of deer on a bright summer evening. Then again, there was an occasion when I was rushing along the pavement, from my house to a side door of the church, dressed as a tramp. I was about to slip in through the door and surprise a lunch gathering with a little drama skit. Just as I approached the door, who should I encounter but the local undertaker? I think we were both too embarrassed to know what to say, although the scope for amusing one-liners was considerable.

Not surprisingly, the closing chapters of Matthew's Gospel are taken up with the death, burial, resurrection and ascension of Jesus. However, tucked in there alongside tearing temple curtains, earthquakes, angels and more, there is an account of what must surely have been the most unusual walks ever witnessed in the city of Jerusalem. After telling us about an earthquake which shook the city, Matthew records the phenomenon of other resurrections.

His description leaves so many unanswered questions. How many of them were there? Did they go to the temple, head for their former homes, or just walk about the city? How long did they stay? Presumably, this was not the start of a second, resurrected life for them – but just a brief appearance. Like the ripped temple curtain and the splitting open of the graves, this was a further sign that God had ruptured the erstwhile order of things in the spectacular act of Christ's resurrection. It is hard to imagine the surprise and shock of those who met these resurrected ones.

Passages like this remind us that our view of God is all too often tame and domesticated. We imagine that he can only do the things he has done before, and that certain rules will be obeyed. There is an incipient arrogance to our belief that we can describe the sum extent of his capabilities. Not a bit of it! Any God who can make an intricate and beautiful world at the sound of his voice and hurl the stars into space knows no limits.

Before you walk anywhere today, stop and ask yourself this question: how surprised would I be if God did something today which I regard as impossible? That impossible thing might be to heal someone, to end a conflict, or even to change your mind! Anything could happen . . .

Prayer

> Dear God, I don't find it easy to believe in the impossible, but I do believe in you. Help me to put those two things together today, and to walk out of here ready to see miracles. Amen.

Walk 56

Levi Walks After Jesus

As he walked along, he saw Levi son of Alphaeus sitting at the tax collector's booth. 'Follow me,' Jesus told him, and Levi got up and followed him.

Mark 2:14

It's not like I hadn't seen it coming. This event had been in the planning for almost two years. The last few months had seen preparations gathering pace, and the previous evening there had been a rehearsal in this very place. All the same, when I stood at the front of St Salvator's Chapel in St Andrews on my wedding day and said the words 'I do', they had a kind of thunderclap effect upon me. In that moment, I realised that these two words would affect every hour of every day for the foreseeable future. The ripple effects of those two words would spread out across the next thirty years in all sorts of wonderful ways. There would be laughter and tears and children and memories and pastorates and adventures and 101 new horizons – all starting with the words 'I do'.

Levi was a tax collector. By exacting taxes from his fellow citizens, he could not only earn a wage from his Roman paymasters, but also cream off a tidy additional profit for himself. On the basis that where the crowds are, there the money will be, he had set up his collection booth on the shores of Lake Galilee. If all went to plan, he would be home that evening with pleasantly full pockets. Of course, it did not. Jesus came by, teaching the crowd as he went, and they were all too enraptured by his teaching to stop for anything as dull as tax payments. Not only that, but Jesus had other plans for Levi, as Mark records in his gospel.

With those two words 'follow me', Levi's life would change out of all recognition. After leaving that tax booth behind, he would witness miracles firsthand, soak up private teaching from Jesus, and ultimately join a small band of people who would begin to change the course of history. It was a good exchange to leave behind the money that he knew for the adventures he could never have imagined. His short walk from his tax booth to Jesus' side would take him into the history books, and we are still reading his story today.

That is exactly the exchange which all of us have made who have opted to follow Jesus. Like him, we have left a kind of certainty behind to embrace a brand of delicious uncertainty whose name is faith. It is happening right now, as you are reading this book. Right now, all over the world, there are people hearing the words of Jesus to 'follow me' and falling in step with him. They know what they are leaving behind, but have precious little idea about what lies ahead. The anxiety of that is eclipsed by the joy of knowing him and being known. All shall be well.

Let there be joy in your footsteps today. Let there be a sense of anticipation about what may be, rather than regret over what is not. Ask God that he might keep your eyes fixed on the road ahead with such keen anticipation, that looking back feels like mere folly.

Prayer

Dear God, I thank you for the day when I heard those same words as Levi: 'Follow me.' Some days I struggle to see where you are going, and occasionally I am reluctant to follow, but I thank you for the faith that keeps me moving. Amen.

Walk 57

Jesus Walks into a Synagogue

Jesus went into the synagogue . . .

Mark 3:1

Back in the days when 'slide shows' were a thing, I would take lots of slides on 35mm film whenever I travelled. Especially if I travelled on any kind of church business, I would be expected to report back to the lovely people in the church who had prayed for me. On this particular occasion, I had been travelling in north-east India as part of a scheme known as the 'Pastor's Book Set Project'.[9] Pastors who had access only to a Bible and hymnbook were being provided with a small library of theological books. Speakers like me were there to offer some training on how best to make use of these resources. My travels had taken me to Guwahati in the state of Assam, and Shillong in the state of Meghalaya. I was about ten minutes into my slide presentation in a darkened church hall, when a visitor arrived. He had cycled to the meeting in the rain, and still had his waterproofs on. Instead of sliding in at the back, he rustled his way right down to the front row, where he took a seat. I think it would be fair to say that every eye (and ear) was upon him.

In our story today, Jesus walks into a synagogue, and every eye is upon him as he does so. Among the people in there were those who were just itching for Jesus to do something wrong of which they could accuse him. His loving interpretation of the will of God and his popularity among the crowds did nothing to endear him to the religious establishment of the day, and maybe some hoped that this would be the beginning of the end for him. When Mark writes quite simply that 'Jesus went into the synagogue' you can almost feel the tension behind those five words. Occasions like this were confrontations, just as Jesus always intended them to be. He knew full well that the authorities would challenge him over the healing he was about to perform, and knew equally well that he would challenge them back. The few steps which it took Jesus to enter the synagogue were steps which took him closer to his crucifixion. Acts like the healing of the man in the congregation would all be held against him when the time came.

I can't read the story of Jesus' brave and defiant walk into that gathering without thinking of my brave sisters and brothers in persecuted churches around the world. Even today, some of them will walk into situations at work or in the street which will one day deprive them of their liberty, and even their lives. Like Jesus before them, they know full well what it will cost them to do the right thing, but they do it anyway. How honoured I am to call such people family.

As you walk today, why not ask God to help you hear those other footsteps? As you place one foot in front of the other to get to where you need to be, think of those whose footsteps for Jesus will lead them into danger. They may be pastors or evangelists, or simply those who have given a clear and public testimony to their faith in Jesus. Like him in the synagogue, they know that every eye is upon them, but still they walk in courage and faith.

Prayer

Dear God, although I don't know their names, I pray for those who will walk into danger on Jesus' behalf today. Give them all the courage and resolve that they might need, I pray. Amen.

Walk 58

A Demoniac Walks Home

Go home to your own people and tell them how much the
Lord has done for you, and how he has had mercy on you.
Mark 5:19

Sometimes the longest journey you ever take is the few steps it takes to make a U-turn. I know because I have done it, and often with a heavy heart. I have had to turn round and head back towards the mess I have created or the dent in fellowship which I have made. It can be an awkward journey.

Mark tells us the story of a deeply troubled man in the fifth chapter of his gospel. This poor man is so wracked by the demons within that he lives as a feral creature, chained among the tombs in the local graveyard. In fact, he is so overwhelmed that his own identity has been subsumed by the demons residing in him. When asked his name, it is the demons who reply that are 'Legion' (Mark 5:9). Untroubled by their number, Jesus casts them out into a herd of pigs, and all 2,000 of them run headlong into the waters of a nearby lake. When the thrashing of the water and the squealing has subsided, the voices of an angry crowd take over, begging Jesus to go away and leave them in peace.

Just before Jesus complies, there is one more conversation. The healed man, now upright and rational for the first time he can remember, stands on the shore and asks if he can go with his Saviour. Jesus refuses, telling him to go home to his own people. While it makes perfect sense in terms of 'spreading the word', it must have seemed harsh at the time.

I often like to reflect on that man's journey home. Were his footsteps light, with the prospect of many a happy reunion, or heavy with the thought that he would not be welcome? As he rounded the last corner, did people quietly shut their doors and children hide behind the skirts of their mothers because the madman was home? Many people would have taken much convincing that he had really changed, and was no longer a monster.

When people make a commitment to Christ and head back home to tell husband or wife or parents or flatmates what they have done, it can be a tough journey. They may anticipate anything from disinterest to ridicule or outright hostility. The important thing to remember is that Jesus who brought about the change can help with the reactions which we encounter towards it. The Saviour who could free this man from his 2,000 demons also knew that the man could handle his journey home, and all that might ensue from it.

Stop, right now, and reflect on those who most need to see the change that Jesus has brought about in you. Next time you head in their direction, ask God to reassure you that he knows what he is doing in sending you there.

Prayer

Dear God, I thank you for those who know me best of all. If I am afraid of their reactions to what you have done within me, then I ask for your help, here and now. Amen.

Walk 59

Jairus Walks Through the Crowd

> He pleaded earnestly with him, 'My little daughter is dying. Please come and put your hands on her so that she will be healed and live.'
>
> *Mark 5:23*

In the room were well over one hundred preachers. None of the people there were unaccustomed to the limelight. Most of them would stand up most weeks in front of a congregation and speak up without a moment's hesitation. So what was the matter with them? It was the second plenary session of this conference of preachers, an invited guest had preached on a gospel passage, and now all were asked for their questions and comments. It was an acutely awkward moment, with not a hand raised nor a question asked. In the end, I did ask a question but felt like I was breaking some kind of unwritten rule by doing so. Even those who thrive in the spotlight don't welcome 'exposure' when it comes in the wrong context.

Jairus was not a shy man. As a leader of the local synagogue, he would have had a public profile and been known to many of his Jewish neighbours. All the same, the experience of pushing through the crowd and then shedding all his dignity as he fell at the feet of Jesus to ask for help must have been acutely awkward. When Mark records the incident, it is as if the man's language has broken down along with his dignity, and in the original text his needs come tumbling out in a barely formed, 'Gotta help me.' The walk from the edge of the crowd to the feet of Jesus not only took him through the bodies gathered there, but it took him from a figure of respect to a desperately needy parent. At the feet of Jesus there is no dignity, only need.

Sometimes I believe we are rather in love with our own view of ourselves. There are certain ways in which we choose to describe ourselves, and certain ways in which we would like others to perceive us. This may be associated with our age, our experience, or our role. While writing this book, I have been coming to terms with no longer being a minister in pastoral charge. Despite all my many years of church life, for the first few weeks I found arriving at my new home church acutely awkward. The reason for my awkwardness was as simple as it was silly: I did not know where to sit. For three and a half decades the place I always sat was at the front – either on the front row or on the platform. Where was I to sit now that I had no 'official' role? In the end my self-important bubble was burst by the kindness of others in the church, who saw the newbie looking awkward and said, 'Do you want to sit with us?'

It may just be that today God needs you to leave a degree of anonymity behind and step up for something. To do so will leave you feeling exposed and awkward. It may even make you feel that you have 'let yourself in' for something. Jairus certainly had. His walk from the edge of the crowd to the feet of Jesus would bring him later to a room in his family home where he would see Jesus take his daughter's hand and raise her from the dead as easily as we might wake somebody from sleeping. His dignity was a small price to pay for a miracle.

Prayer

> Dear God, I can see where I need to be today. It is not far away, just a few steps, really, but the walk between here and there frightens the life out of me. Call me again, I pray, and this time, may I have the courage to follow. Amen.

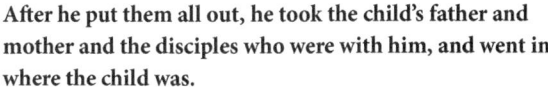

Walking Across the Threshold

After he put them all out, he took the child's father and mother and the disciples who were with him, and went in where the child was.

Mark 5:40

I was a new and very inexperienced pastor, with so much to learn. For the first time in my life, I had spent the afternoon with someone who was dying. As late afternoon slipped into evening, the end came for him, and I stayed on with his widow in another room as we waited for a district nurse to come. When the nurse came, she poked her head around the door and asked if I would come with her to verify the destruction of various medications, which I was happy to do. Maybe seeing how young and green I was, she said that presumably I had never seen a dead body before, and would I like to step into the room with her? I am not sure if 'like' was the word, but I was very grateful for her gentle help.

We last met Jairus in the previous chapter. You may remember him as a desperate father who pushed through the crowd to get to Jesus, and then begged him to heal his little girl. We left the story at that point, but now we have arrived at his house. Outside there is a crowd of mourners wailing and crying. Jesus hushes them with news that the little girl is not dead but sleeping, which simply turns their wailing to derision. At this point, he asks the little girl's parents, together with Peter, James and John, to walk into the house with him. Can you imagine the feeling as they crossed the threshold? Outside was a noisy and now agitated crowd, inside was sombre stillness, and the prospect of seeing a dead child laid out before them. All the same, we read that they 'went in where the child was'.

Sometimes we have to go to the darkest places to see the brightest miracle. Even if Peter, James and John recoiled from the prospect of what they might see inside that room, they had to go there in order to see what Jesus would do. In fact, they would see him take the child's hand, speak words which were the equivalent of 'up you get, poppet' and watch as the girl walked around the room. Years later, when Peter would be called on to work similar miracles, he must have been so glad that he had been there. For him and his fellow disciples, that short walk across the threshold was a walk from fear to celebration, and from doubt to faith.

My walk of faith has certainly taken me to some uncomfortable places. On one occasion I had to visit an inmate in the hospital wing of his prison. The journey from prison gate to visiting room must have taken a full fifteen minutes, with all the locking and unlocking of gates. Once there, the warder locked me in with the prisoner, pointed at the alarm button and said, 'Any problems, give us a shout. I'll be back in half an hour or so.' To say that I felt nervous would be an understatement. However, as with Peter, James and John, the reserve of faith draws upon the things you have seen before. Once you have crossed one threshold in pursuit of God, it is easier to cross the next.

What are some of the hardest places to which your faith has taken you? They may include hospital beds, youth clubs, street corners, or even the front room to share a cup of tea with a person who is raging against God. If you can look back on them, then it clearly means that you survived them! Take some time on your walk today to thank God for his sustaining strength in those situations.

Prayer

Dear God, I have to admit today that there are places to which I have followed you only reluctantly. They have been hard and I have been afraid. All the same, you have strengthened me and helped me through them, for which I thank you. Amen.

Walk 61

Up the Mountain with Jesus

Jesus took Peter, James and John with him and led them up a high mountain . . .

Mark 9:2

I never wanted to be the one asking the question, but I always hoped that somebody would. I would sit at the back of the maths class, as far out of the teacher's eyeline as I could possibly get, and stare in a sort of quiet desperation at the calculation he had written on the blackboard. When another hand would shoot up the other side of the room and announce, 'Sir, I don't get it', I would breathe a grateful sigh of relief. Thank goodness somebody had asked the question.

I sometimes wonder if Peter, James and John were exchanging similar glances of desperation in today's story – each of them willing the other to speak up and ask what on earth was going on. Things had been going so well recently, with crowds of people fed and dramatic miracles of every kind. Now was a time to stay visible, surely? And yet, Mark writes that Jesus took them away up the mountain.

As we have the whole story, we know they were in for a treat. Up at the top of the mountain, they would see the spectacular glory of Jesus in a way that none of them had seen before. In a moment of heavenly radiance, they would see him flanked by Moses and Elijah – thereby confirming his place as the fulfilment of the patriarchal hopes and prophetic promises. As if that weren't enough, God himself would come to them in a cloud on the mountaintop, confirming the identity of Jesus and telling them to listen to him. The thing is, none of them *knew* that at this point. All they knew was that they were leaving behind the opportunities and the needs down below for a mysterious trip to the mountaintop.

Where I live, I have only to leave the house to see mountains in the distance. Sometimes they are barely discernible from the sky, in a blue-grey haze. Other times, they have brushes of snow and stand out from far away. Up close, it becomes apparent that even the smallest of them constitutes a long and serious climb. If somebody asked me to climb one of them without telling me why, I would have plenty of time to wonder about the reasons on the way up.

There are times in our walk of faith where it is essential that we should not know where we are going, nor why we have been called there. Without that, it becomes all about the going and not about the trusting. It was Martin Luther who described discipleship as a journey of bewilderment: 'Bewilderment is the true comprehension. Not to know where you are going is the true knowledge.'[10] Like those three disciples, walking unknowing up the mountain, there are times when we just have to follow our heavenly guide and not ask the reasons why.

When you walk today, why not reflect on those moments in your own journey of faith where you felt least certain about what was going on? It may have been the time that you were called to leave one job without knowing where the next one might be found. It may have been the time when you felt called to move from one place to another with no firm plan about how life might be when you got there. These are moments of true faith and are to be treasured.

Prayer

Dear God, when I look back just now, I can see moments when I had no more idea what you were up to than Peter, James and John did in this story. I was sure neither where we were going nor why the climb was so steep. I thank you for your sustaining power in those moments, and for the glimpses of your glory along the way. Amen.

Walk 62

Bartimaeus Follows On

'Go,' said Jesus, 'your faith has healed you.' Immediately he received his sight and followed Jesus along the road.

Mark 10:52

There is a young woman whose account I follow on social media, who is blind.[11] Most days she posts a video about some aspect of her life without sight, usually with her trusty cane by her side. Sometimes she demonstrates how she goes about the simplest tasks, such as choosing an outfit or boiling an egg, without being able to see what she is doing. Other days she answers the questions which sighted people would like to ask a blind person but have felt unable to do so. All of this she does with a charm and humanity which reaches out to her many followers. When asked what she would most like to see if her sight were restored, she said that it would be faces. I wonder what I would most miss?

In Mark 10 we meet Bartimaeus, who is blind. Unlike other stories in the Gospels, we don't know how long he has been in this state, but we do know that he is keen to get out of it. Hearing the commotion when Jesus is passing on his way through Jericho, he cries out to ask for his help. Even when the crowd try to hush him, he is not to be put off, and continues to cry out. Jesus hears, the man is summoned to his side, and his sight is restored on the spot. At this point, Jesus tells him that he can go. If that were me, I wonder where I would have wanted to go first?

Would I have wanted to stride back up the middle of the road where everybody had seen me as a beggar? Would I have wanted to seek out family and friends to show them that the most wonderful miracle had happened? Would I have wanted to rush to the nearest marketplace and *see* the fruit which I could only pick out before by smell and touch? Despite Jesus' kind dismissal, which gave the man permission to leave, we read instead that he 'followed Jesus along the road' (Mark 10:52). We don't know where they went nor how long he followed him for, but we do know that despite all the other possibilities, his instinct made him take his first sighted steps with the one who had healed him.

Although I have expressed my thanks to Jesus at many times and in many ways, it all feels a little insipid compared to this man's clear instinct to follow him wherever he may go. My praise is sometimes a little too polite and my worship a little too convenient. I fit them in around other things, rather than trimming my life to fit them. This man, with his instinctive walk, makes me rethink those choices.

Why not ask God for a little reckless gratitude on your walk today? Why not ask that he remind you again quite how great is the transformation that he has wrought in your life? The difference between *then* and *now* is as great as that between death and life, or darkness and light, if we could but see it. Ask for his help, as Bartimaeus did.

Prayer

Dear God, please forgive me that I have forgotten how great a change you have brought to my life. When I found you, as Bartimaeus did at the roadside, everything changed. Remind me of that today, I pray. Amen.

Walk 63

Jesus Walks into the Garden

When they had sung a hymn, they went out to the Mount of Olives.

Mark 14:26

All my life he had been a prisoner. There had been campaigns about him, concerts in his name, and his picture was on 1,000 T-shirts. When he walked down the driveway of Pollsmoor Prison, accompanied by the president of South Africa, I felt that Nelson Mandela's walk was something I just had to watch. It felt as if every single footstep were a 'notch' in history, and should be witnessed.

Those familiar with the events of the first Easter week will know that the Last Supper was followed by a walk to the Mount of Olives. Mark describes it with characteristic simplicity.

There would follow heartfelt prayer, disappointment, arrest and forcible removal by soldiers. Before that, though, there is a world of meaning in that little word 'out'. Jerusalem was a walled city at the time, and Jesus could not have accessed the Mount of Olives without exiting through one of the city gates. Above each would have been a carving in the stonework of a vine. The vine was supposed to represent the fruitfulness of God's special, chosen people. In fact, that vine had withered and failed, as generation after generation ignored the prophets. The fact that God's Messiah could walk unnoticed through the gate and beneath such a carving was proof of how far things had slipped from the way they should have been. The footsteps of Jesus below it, like the footsteps of Mandela up that dusty prison drive, echoed with deep significance.

Do you sometimes find that your footsteps are accompanied by another, unwelcome, journey as you walk? Do you find yourself rather too aware of the journeys which should have been and the paths which might have been a better choice? For regrets to intrude into our thoughts unbidden is inevitable. However, it is up to us how much houseroom we give them.

Here's a suggestion. Should you find that such regrets make an appearance into your walk today, do not try to push them away. Do not dismiss them out of hand, but rather allow them to breathe. Take some time to tell God about them, to confess where confession is needed, and to entrust the onward journey to him. Jesus, who walked beneath that vine of disappointment on the city gateway, knows all about unfulfilled plans. Thankfully, he knows all about how to triumph despite them too.

Prayer

> Dear God, if I think about it too much, I am sure I would be reminded of all sorts of ways that I have let you down. I don't want to be overwhelmed by it, but I don't want to ignore it, either. As we walk and talk today, maybe we could take a look at those things, at least a bit? Amen.

Walk 64

Simon Walks Beneath a Cross

 A certain man from Cyrene, Simon, the father of Alexander and Rufus, was passing by on his way in from the country, and they forced him to carry the cross.

Mark 15:21

The world loves heroes. It loves local heroes, have-a-go heroes and accidental heroes. That said, the word itself suggests that a person has *chosen* to do something heroic, to 'step up' and transcend their normal boundaries in the interests of a greater need or cause. Can a person be said to be a hero if they have no choice in the matter?

In the case of Simon of Cyrene, that is exactly what happens. Although Matthew, Mark and Luke all mention him in their Gospels, and all with slightly different details, nobody suggests he actually *chose* to carry the cross for Jesus. In fact, Luke even states he was 'seized' by the Roman guard detail accompanying Jesus to the place of crucifixion (Luke 23:26). He had come into the city of Jerusalem from distant Cyrene (modern Libya) with his own business in mind, and definitely not intending to carry the cross for the Messiah.

In the centuries since, Simon has been turned into a cipher for faithful, humble service to Jesus. He has been held up to Christians for generations as an example of servanthood, and the embodiment of Christ's injunction to 'take up [our] cross' (Matt. 16:24). Can that really be so, though, when he was not a volunteer?

Maybe your footsteps today will take you on a path you did not choose. You have to go to *that* place and do *that* thing, even though your heart sinks at the very prospect. A rational part of you knows that it may be useful, but your emotional self is screaming out that it is unfair, unwarranted and very definitely unwelcome. You have no more choice in the matter than Simon did of old. What if your reticent actions have as much impact as his did, though? What if your journey today ends up inspiring someone else to walk a hard road and do a good thing?

Although we cannot be certain, it is likely that there is more to this story. Since Mark mentions Simon's sons Alexander and Rufus by name, it is likely that they were known to Mark's audience in the early church. Did Simon go back and tell his sons of the king whose cross he was obliged to carry? Maybe he stayed on at the crest of the hill and heard Jesus cry out in a loud voice 'It is finished' (John 19:30), watching then as the sky darkened and the earth shook? We shall never know, but clearly the impact of this day lingered on. Simon's reluctant walk led to all kinds of interesting places.

Prayer

Dear God, you know that I don't want to do this thing today. It wasn't my idea, and my heart feels heavy at the very prospect. Please help me on my way, and maybe even use my footsteps for the good of others, as you did with Simon. Amen.

Walk 65

Mary Walks to Elizabeth

> Mary got ready and hurried to a town in the hill country of Judea [to visit Elizabeth] . . .
>
> **Luke 1:39**

I am pretty sure the word 'adulting' is a recent invention. I definitely don't remember hearing it when I was leaving the nursery slopes of adolescence and heading up the mountain of adulthood. All the same, I hear it quite often now. I hear it when parents talk about their children learning to be independent at university and beyond. I hear it when young adults talk about the dubious pleasures of agreeing a mortgage or paying tax. 'Adulting' is the sense that you are taking on tasks and responsibilities which hitherto have been seen by you as the province of older and wiser people. In short, it is growing up. Whenever we tackle something new, strange and scary, it is helpful to know that somebody else has been there before us.

Mary was a young woman, maybe even in her teens, and had been charged with a terrifying responsibility. Not only was she to become a mother, which is a responsibility of epic proportions, but she was to become mother to God's Messiah. Thankfully, in the very same moment that she received this incredible news, she was also told that her elderly relative Elizabeth was also miraculously pregnant. Elizabeth was six months further on than Mary and could doubtless give some comfort and advice. Luke writes that immediately after the angel's visit Mary set off in a hurry.

I wonder why she hurried? I suspect it was because she did not want to spend another second sitting alone with this momentous news. She needed people with her, and her own relative could not have been a more fitting person. As Mary made her way to her relative's house there must have been 101 questions going through her mind. How did Elizabeth find out? Was she scared too? Did she feel ready? In times of great anxiety, the presence of those who have been there before us can be an enormous source of strength.

Every time I read this story, I smile at the fact that the angel *told* Mary about her relative, even though there was no prompting of any part on Mary's side. Neither woman *had* to know about the other in order for God's plan to be fulfilled, and yet he knew they would need each other. God the Father knew how Mary would be feeling, and instructed his angel to provide some reassurance. Elizabeth was God's provision to Mary, just as Elizabeth's son would one day be a help to Mary's son.

If you are going to walk alone today, they why not imagine some company around you? Try to call to mind the faces and the voices of those who have been of such help to you along the way. They may have stepped into your path just as you were starting out as a Christian believer, or they may have fallen in step with you at the moment when you were bearing a heavy burden. Either way, they have been God's provision to you. Although they are not with you right now, cherish their company in your mind as you walk. Give thanks to God for all that they have brought to you.

Prayer

> Dear God, how I thank you for those men and women whom I have named before you just now. I thank you for the strength, encouragement and joy that they have brought to me. Wherever their feet may fall today, may you go before them, I pray. Amen.

Walk 66

Mary and Joseph Walk to Bethlehem

He went there to register with Mary . . .

Luke 2:5

I had waited a long time for this moment, more than fifty-seven years, in fact. Seven months before, I had paid a holding deposit to buy a house overlooking the Irish Sea in Wales. At the time, the house had only a few courses of brick work, no windows, no roof and no upstairs. Now, it was all complete, and I was walking from my car to the solicitor's office to sign the final paperwork. That done, I would transfer the largest amount of money I had ever moved anywhere into the relevant bank account, and the house would be mine. A dream long cherished and a plan long hatched was becoming reality, and it all felt pretty scary.

By the time we reach our story today, a very long plan is under way. It is a plan as old as Eden itself, when God promised that one day he would put things right. Mary has been told that she is to bear the Messiah, God's Son. Joseph has been informed of God's plan too. Now, they must make their way to Bethlehem, the city where the world-changing event of the Messiah's birth is to happen. Luke describes their departure from their hometown of Nazareth in the simplest terms.

This was no short walk, since the distance was some ninety miles. At this point we should probably dismiss from our minds their faithful donkey companion, stock-in-trade of so many Nativity plays. If they were wealthy enough to own a donkey, or fortunate enough to borrow one, the chances are that it would have been carrying their luggage rather than either of them.

So here we have two people, one of them heavily pregnant, walking ninety miles along rough roads and across country. Doubtless they would have talked some of the time, but there would also have been times of quiet. After all, both of them were dealing with their part in a scenario bigger than humanity itself. How could you put that into words?

I am so grateful that God does not always expect me to be articulate when I talk to him. I live my life by words, either written or broadcast, and yet sometimes I find that the things I want to tell him about leave me awkward and tongue-tied. When praying for people in desperate need, or looking at a world in indescribable turmoil, words simply do not seem adequate. In those moments I feel for this couple, Mary and Joseph, making their long and taxing way to Bethlehem and wondering what it all would mean.

Right now, before you walk anywhere, why not call to mind some of the deepest needs which seem almost too big for words? For the duration of this walk, you can carry them in your mind and offer them to God, no words required.

Prayer

Dear God, what a long walk that must have seemed to Mary and Joseph. I thank you that you accompanied them all through those miles and saw them safely to the next bit of the story. As we walk today, help me to talk to you about the biggest things that trouble me, even if I don't use a single word. Amen.

Walk 67

The Shepherds Walk Down from the Hills

> When the angels had left them and gone into heaven, the shepherds said to one another, 'Let's go to Bethlehem and see this thing that has happened, which the Lord has told us about.'
>
> *Luke 2:15*

'Who, me?' Those were the words in my head as I closed the front door quietly behind me in the early darkness of an October morning. Waiting at the kerbside was a BBC car waiting to whisk me off to Central London for a live radio broadcast. As I got into the plush back seats, a little voice inside me said, 'This kind of thing happens to other people, not to me.' It was all a bit unreal, to be honest.

Some of the most beloved characters in any depiction of the Christmas story are the shepherds. They were far from beloved in their day, though. Living outside for most of the time meant that they were both ritually and physically unclean. Whenever they did come down from the hills into the town, people would probably cross the road to avoid them. All this makes it especially amazing that God should have chosen them as the first people beyond Mary and Joseph to be made aware of the Messiah's birth. It was for them that the skies above Jerusalem were crowded with an angelic choir heralding the good news.

When the angels had gone, an eerie silence must have descended on that star-lit hill. Maybe they looked at each other with arched eyebrows as if to say, 'Did that really happen?' Maybe they just stared off into the skies as if the angels might come back again. Whatever their immediate response, it did not last, as Luke records. They must have walked down that road with a swagger and a spring in their step such as they had never known before. They had been chosen, picked out, selected by God's divine purpose to be let in on the greatest event of all time. I imagine they were telling their children and grandchildren about it until their dying day.

Of course, there are times when our footsteps as Christians should be slow, reflective and even heavy. It is right and proper that sometimes our walk with God should be with head bowed and a keen awareness of our sin. That should not always be the case, though. Sometimes our hearts should soar as we realise that we have been chosen, and those words which were in my head on that October morning should be ours: who, me?

When I first came to faith, George Wade Robinson's words from 'Loved with Everlasting Love' would often echo in my mind, especially when out in the countryside:

> Heaven above is softer blue,
> Earth around is sweeter green;
> Something lives in every hue
> Christless eyes have never seen . . . [12]

God had put an undeniable spring in my step.

How's your step today? Before you go anywhere, why not stop and ask God to wake up in you once again the sense of wonder that he should love you? Do it now, without a moment's hesitation.

Prayer

Dear God, how light the hearts of those shepherds must have been as they walked along, to know that they were so special to you. Today, I ask that you would remind me that I am special in your sight too. Amen.

Walk 68

Walking in a Panic

> When they did not find him, they went back to Jerusalem to look for him. After three days they found him in the temple courts...
>
> *Luke 2:45–46*

When it comes to parents and children, there is a fine line between independence and disobedience. The perception of it may depend upon which side of the generation gap you stand! As a small boy, I was on holiday with my parents in an old seaside resort. Together with my brother, we were out for a walk along the seafront. As far as I was concerned, my decision to scramble down and walk between the beach huts and the sea wall, instead of sticking to the path, was an act of independence. My parents, I suspect, saw it differently. When they got to the end of the path and there was no sign of me, panic set in on both parts. Thankfully, we were reunited very soon. Years later, when I momentarily lost my son in the aisles of a French supermarket, I understood something of what my poor parents must have gone through.

Think of the awesome responsibility which was entrusted to Mary and Joseph during Jesus' childhood years. After the starlight and fanfare of Christmas night, there were many summers and winters to come before Jesus would be seen by the world for who he was. All that time, their responsibility was to nurture him, love him and keep him safe. Each year, they would take him with them and the extended family on a trip from Nazareth to the great temple in Jerusalem for the Passover celebrations. Imagine their irrepressible panic when they got part-way home and realised that he was missing. Luke tells us that they retraced their steps, and took three days to find him.

Those three days must have been a whirlwind of panic and searching as they walked back and forth along the route, frantically searching for the precious boy who had been entrusted to them. As night fell on the first and second days, both heart and feet must have been so sore. God had given them this charge, after all, and they were failing at it. I suspect that the only thing keeping hope alive was the angel's promise to Mary that 'He will be great' (Luke 1:32). That is a promise that could not be fulfilled if he were lost, so in the end all would be well. In the end, of course, it was. The 12-year-old Jesus was reunited with Mary and Joseph, and they continued the journey home together.

There are times in all our lives when the tide of panic within rises so high as to almost drown us. When that happens, the only thing to do is to hold onto the promises that we have already been given. They become our reassurance that all is well, despite evidence to the contrary. While I am in the course of writing this book, I am also engaged in the business of learning how to fly a glider. At those moments when flight seems all but impossible and the ground looks scarily far away beneath me, I look at the airspeed indicator and it reminds me that there is enough speed to keep the plane aloft, whatever my fevered imagination may be telling me to the contrary!

Prayer

Dear God, today the problem is not so much that I have lost my way as that I have lost sight of it. I can't see where I am going, and I panic that all is lost. Reunite me with my purpose, just as you reunited Mary and Joseph with Jesus, I pray. Amen.

Walk 69

Jesus Walks from the Brink

He walked right through the crowd and went on his way.
Luke 4:30

I am not a big fan of Formula 1, I have to say. At least on the television, I find the whole thing very repetitive, as the cars go round and round the track. That said, if there is ever a crash, I find myself watching with a kind of horrible fascination. Those fragile cars bounce and cartwheel across the tracks with pieces flying in all directions, and frequently burst into flames on impact with the sidewall. Whenever I see the driver climb out of the vehicle and walk upright through the flames to safety, my spirit soars. How can that even be possible?

Today we visit a dark corner of the gospel story. It is dark because we see Jesus rejected by the very people who might have given him the warmest welcome – the residents of his hometown. It is also dark because we see the naked ugliness of mob violence at its worst. Jesus' words in the local synagogue have offended people so badly that they drive him from the building and manhandle him to the edge of town. As if that were not bad enough, a kind of bestial anger takes over, and they push and shove Jesus to the top of a local cliff, ready to throw him down from it. It is the kind of moment we might watch through interlaced fingers in a movie, if we watched it at all. Before it had scarcely begun, Jesus' ministry might have ended in a crumpled and bloodied heap at the foot of that cliff. Thankfully, it was not to be, and Luke writes that he walked through the crowd and went on his way.

What on earth was that walk like, I wonder? Did people look at the ground as he passed, suddenly aware of the visceral violence which had overtaken them? Perhaps they let him through only reluctantly, deliberately jabbing shoulders in his way and forcing him to push them aside. Maybe the crowd parted, like the waves of old before Moses in the Red Sea. However it was, Jesus walked through entirely unharmed, and went onto the city of Capernaum, where he did great things.

Whenever we hear the name of Jesus taken in vain, or hear him belittled, we should return to this picture of him in Luke's Gospel. We should look him square in the face as he walks through the crowd with no more fear than a child pushing aside long wisps of grass as they run through a field. This is Jesus, on a mission, divinely called, mightily protected and entirely unabashed. He is a figure of admiration, not sympathy, and deserves respect, not pity.

Maybe as you walk today, you will find yourself remembering how some of those who do not know him as you do have mocked Jesus. Don't worry about him – he can look after himself. Instead, think of them. If you can, bring the sight of their faces and the sound of their voices to mind as you pray for them today. Jesus loves them every bit as much as he did the members of that angry crowd and would love to see them know that for themselves.

Prayer

Dear God, there have been times when my heart is all but broken as I think of the way people dismiss you. Their harsh and unconsidered words cut me deeply. Help me to remember this picture of you in Nazareth today, and to pray for them from my heart. Amen.

Walk 70

A Widow's Son Walks

The dead man sat up and began to talk, and Jesus gave him back to his mother.

Luke 7:15

One of the issues about training for ministry in a part-time, or church-based way, was that I missed out on some of the field trips that my fellow students were having. Where I felt that gap was especially marked, it was up to me to cover those things for myself. All of which meant that I landed up walking through a door at the back of a crematorium chapel into a world seen by few. My local undertaker had arranged the trip for me, and as we passed through the door a little bit of me rather wished he hadn't! I need not have worried. The crematorium steward was a lovely man, who brought both compassion and professionalism to his task. Accompanied by him, I witnessed every single bit of the process, from the moment when a coffin disappears out of sight in the chapel, to the moment when an urn of ashes is ready for collection. I was struck by the meticulous care which was taken, but also with the finality of it all. Any person, rich or poor, great or small, is reduced to the same at this point.

As Jesus was passing through the town of Nain, with a large crowd at his side, he encountered another crowd. This one was not joyful, like his. At its head was a widow who was making her way out of the town with her dead son on a bier, ready to bury him. Moved by the sight, Jesus told her not to cry, and made his way to the bier with the young man's body on it. As the astonished bearers stood still, Jesus told the dead man to get up, which he duly did. At this point, Luke records that Jesus 'gave him back to his mother' and then moved on.

While I love this story in the gospel, and can feel the crackle of power in the crowd and the tidal wave of relief for that widowed mother, there is a bit of me that wants to call out every time I read it, 'But what happened next?' Presumably the Jesus crowd and the funeral crowd mingled at this point, babbling excitedly and jostling to get a glimpse of the young man who had been on his way to the graveyard just a few moments before. What after that, though? At some point after the excitement had died down, the mother and son must have started to make their way home. For her, she was retracing a path which she had trodden in such a different way earlier that day. For him, even the act of placing one foot in front of the other to walk was something which he had thought he would never do again. Every step on the homeward walk was a miracle – for both of them in different ways.

We would probably all walk a little differently today had we witnessed such a thing. However, these stories are intended to feed our faith even now. Take a little time on your walk today to dwell on this or some of the other miracles of Jesus. In his company, you walk in the shadow of a person who can turn water into wine, make the blind see and raise the dead to life. Don't forget it!

Prayer

> Dear God, I thank you for this story and others like it. Help me to remember that you are still just as powerful today. Amen.

Walk 71

A Meal Interrupted

A woman in that town who lived a sinful life learned that Jesus was eating at the Pharisee's house, so she came there with an alabaster jar of perfume.

Luke 7:37

It was a beautiful setting for a lunch in the open air. To one side were the blue waters of a deep lake, held back by an elegant curving dam over which we had just driven. All around were the mountains of the French Jura, some of the bigger ones fading into the blue haze on this perfect day. Settled with our drinks, we were just reaching for the fries when it happened. A car had come hurtling across the dam, taken the corner too sharply and slammed into one of the concrete planters at the edge of the restaurant. Thankfully no one was hurt, but it will forever be the thing I remember most about that meal.

Simon the Pharisee had landed a major catch when Jesus accepted his invitation to dinner. While he was not to everybody's taste, the whole town was alive with talk about him, and here he was at Simon's table! Everything was going smoothly, when the meal was interrupted. A woman known locally because of her sinful life gate-crashed the party at his house and 'came there with an alabaster jar of perfume'. After that, things went from bad to worse, with her anointing Jesus, crying on his feet, loosing her hair (which was an unacceptable thing to do in public at the time) and then drying them with it. In the end, Jesus would explain that a good and beautiful thing had happened, rather than a shameful one, but it would have taken some living down on Simon's part.

Every time I read the story, I think about this woman whose courage drove her through the door into Simon's house to perform this extraordinary act of devotion. Did she walk past the house a few times, I wonder, spying out who was sat where? Did she pause just before walking in? If it were me, I think I would have gone around the block at least three or four times carrying that precious jar of perfume, before I dared to go in. There would have been 100 voices in my head telling me not to do such a foolish thing and asking me whatever people would think of me. Thank God she prevailed. Her beautiful act of devotion has stood as an example of reckless and extravagant worship for centuries. Every time our thanks to God seem insipid or our praise seems bland, we have only to look to her example for inspiration.

The history of the church is populated by those who dared to do things for God that others would have found too extravagant, dangerous, or shocking. They have crossed oceans and borders, faced death and danger, stood up to powerful people who wanted to silence them, all because their love for Jesus compelled them to. When they get to heaven, I have a feeling that they and this woman will recognise each other instantly. They will see in each other a spark of defiant faith and courage which sets them apart.

Often on these walks we spend time thanking God for those who have strengthened us or encouraged us, or stood with us in some way. Today, though, I suggest something a little more adventurous. How about using the walk to ask God that we might not just be in awe of those people, but that we might *be* those people? It is a dangerous prayer to pray, but the results might be spectacular!

Prayer

> Lord, sometimes I quake inside when I read of those who have done incredibly brave things for you. I like to shrink into a corner so I can admire their courage from a safe distance. Today, I am going a step further and asking that you would make me courageous too, no matter where it may take me. Amen.

Walk 72

The Twelve Walk Out on a Mission

So they set out and went from village to village, proclaiming the good news and healing people everywhere.

Luke 9:6

I had looked forward to this day so much. I had imagined it and rehearsed it in my head so many times. I had worked and studied and planned for it for years. Over the course of the last thirty-six hours, my parents and I had travelled up through the country, stopping overnight in the Lake District, and now we were here in Fife. After several trips up and down to my new study bedroom, the car was empty and it was time to say goodbye. They would head south to Berkshire, and I would head upstairs to my landing, hoping to remember all those things I had been taught about how to make friends quickly in Freshers' Week. As much as I had wanted this moment to come, there was a sick feeling in the pit of my stomach as I saw the amber indicator on the back of Dad's car flashing to turn left, and it disappeared out of sight.

Jesus had never given anyone to understand that he would be a one-man band. Of course, only he could be the Messiah, but the work of the kingdom would be shared work. The disciples, who had watched him and heard his stories, who had seen the miracles and heard his private teaching on what the parables meant, would one day have to step up and carry the kingdom message for themselves. They had known it was coming. And yet, it must have been a shock when Jesus gathered twelve of them together and told them to go out, acting on his authority and proclaiming his kingdom. As if that weren't bad enough, he told them that they were to take next to nothing with them – no spare luggage or food for the journey – God would provide. Pep-talk over, he sent them out. In his gospel, Luke baldly recalls the moment with the simple words 'So they set out'.

How must that have felt, I wonder? It was one thing to witness the miracles of Jesus, or to drink in his wonderful stories and to lap up his private 'teach-in's about them, but those days were behind them for this next phase. They were now representatives of the kingdom, and of the King himself. Would they remember what they had seen and heard? Would they be able to speak with power and conviction, as their Master had done before them? People would measure the value of the kingdom by the qualities of these disciples, as they are still doing now.

Every once in a while, it does us no harm to recognise the sheer enormity of the task which Jesus has entrusted to us. This should neither overwhelm nor incapacitate us, but rather it should drive us to our knees, asking for more courage, further anointing and a greater awareness of his Spirit's presence with us. It is in such a way, and only in such a way, that we shall find ourselves able to fulfil the task that he has given to us.

Wherever you set out today, you do so as an ambassador for Christ. You walk and talk and speak for him in all you do. Why not ask right now that God might make you aware of that sobering truth with every footstep you take today?

Prayer

> Dear God, every time I realise quite what you have entrusted to people like me, I shudder a little inside. Why would you do such a thing? And yet, I know that you have. Make me aware today of the size of the task, and the far greater size of the one who has entrusted it to me. Amen.

Walk 73

Martha Walks from the Kitchen

> Lord, don't you care that my sister has left me to do the work by myself? Tell her to help me!
>
> *Luke 10:40*

When my brother and I were little, we used to argue an awful lot. We could argue about Lego bricks, cassette tapes, the last cake in the tin, or even whether territory between our two toy garages on the landing was equally distributed. In this, I am sure we were not unusual. Plenty of brothers argue when they are growing up, and quite a few continue it on into adulthood. Thankfully, that has not been the case with us. However, when the 'hostilities' were at their height, I can remember my father advising me that I should 'learn to walk away from an argument'. It was good advice.

It would appear to be advice which Martha could not heed when Jesus came to her house. Not only did the arrival of a stranger place a burden upon her to provide hospitality, but her sister was doing nothing to help. As Martha went to and fro with her preparations for her guest, Mary just sat at Jesus' feet and soaked it all in. In the end, Martha's patience snapped and she walked up to Jesus to tell him exactly what she thought about the situation.

Those who are familiar with the story will know that he did not side with Martha. In fact, he commended Mary for her rapt attention, despite the fact that Martha was doing exactly what culture and religion demanded of her.

There are times when I have felt the need to 'walk up to' someone, as Martha did to Jesus, with something difficult to say. I don't like it. In fact, I hate it. My mouth turns dry, my feet turn to lead and this usually articulate person starts to babble incoherently. If we were to make comparisons, then I think Martha probably managed it with far more dignity than I have ever done.

I wonder whether there is something you need to say to Jesus today, no matter how difficult? You may find that the physical action of walking helps you to untangle it enough to know what it is you need to say. Bear in mind that the thing you have to say cannot possibly catch him off guard. He will be no more surprised by your words than he was by those of Martha. He truly does know us better than we know ourselves.

Prayer

> Lord, there is this difficult thing that I need to say to you today. I am not proud of it, and I almost feel I should not be saying it – but you know it already. As I explain it now, help me to know your presence and hear your voice, I pray. Amen.

Walk 74

One of Ten Walks Back

One of them, when he saw he was healed, came back, praising God in a loud voice.

Luke 17:15

As a minister, I never liked Mothering Sunday. There we are, I have said it in writing, and it feels like a bit of an admission. I never liked it because it is an emotional minefield, which can explode without careful handling. On any given Mothering Sunday, the church may contain those who are mothers and don't like it, those who aren't mothers but would like to be, those who love their mothers, those who don't love their mothers and those who have lost their mothers. Over three and a half decades in church ministry, I am sure I never quite got it right. However, there is one precious Mothering Sunday moment which I shall always treasure.

The service was over, posies of flowers had been distributed to every woman in the congregation, and we were clearing up. As we did so, a member of the team who had created the beautiful posies came up and presented me with one. She explained that 'as pastor, you are like a mother to us, because you care for us'. I almost wept at the time and have done on occasions when I remember it even now. It means a lot to be thanked.

In our story today, Jesus is travelling along the border between Samaria and Galilee, teaching and performing miracles as he goes. On entering one of the villages, he encounters ten lepers living on the outskirts. Not daring to approach him, they call out from a distance, asking him for healing. He grants their request, telling them to go and show themselves to the priest. As they begin to head that way, so the disease that had blighted their lives falls away. Nine of them carry on in the direction of the priest, but the tenth does not. Luke writes that when he saw that he was healed he 'came back, praising God in a loud voice' and threw himself at the feet of Jesus.

When I meet Luke in heaven, I shall ask him for a little more detail here. Did the man run back, I wonder, as if he simply couldn't get there fast enough to thank his healer? Did he walk back slowly, turning his arms this way and that, as if to wonder at a skin which was clean and clear for the first time that he could ever remember? He maybe even stopped along the way so that people who had avoided him as an outcast could see him now free to walk among them. However he came back, the important thing is that he did. We teach children when they are growing up that 'please' and 'thank you' are essential skills to remember. As adult children of God, we so often remember only the first of those two. He may not have healed us from leprosy, but our every prayer for forgiveness, salvation and eternal life has been granted. Those things are true even on our worst day.

Before you go anywhere today, get a piece of paper small enough to slip into your pocket, and write down some of those things for which you want to thank God. They might be great or small. They may apply to every Christian believer or specifically to you. Just write them down, and then carry them with you as you walk. Take time on your walk to thank God for every single one of them. If that means you need to take a slightly longer route, or even to go round again, so be it. I am sure you will find it to be a good use of your time.

Prayer

Dear God, there must be 1,001 things for which I should thank you today. Please help me to remember some of them, so that I can walk thankfully today. Amen.

Walk 75

Zaccheus Takes a Short Walk

> When Jesus reached the spot, he looked up and said to him, 'Zacchaeus, come down immediately. I must stay at your house today.' So he came down at once and welcomed him gladly.
>
> *Luke 19:5-6*

Have you ever been on one of those walks where you feel the sense of other people's eyes 'boring into you'? I can think of two in my own life. The first was when I walked down the aisle of Newbury Baptist Church after concluding my last service there as minister. In fact, it was the last service I ever conducted as a minister in pastoral charge. As I made my way down the aisle, I could not really decide whether to look people in the eye or avert my gaze. I probably ended up doing both. The second walk was at a Baptist assembly – a gathering of hundreds of Baptists from all over the country. I had arrived with a small delegation from the church I was leading at the time, and we had been sitting together for the session in question. When I got up at the end, and responded to a call to seek out prayer for my life and ministry at the front of the auditorium, I could feel their eyes on me with every step. Whatever must they have thought, I wondered?

In chapter 19 of his gospel, Luke tells the story of Zacchaeus – a corrupt and wealthy tax collector. Luke also tells us that he was 'short' (v. 3), so the only way for him to see Jesus on a crowded street was to climb up a sycamore tree. When the moment came, Jesus stopped beneath the tree and 'looked up [at] him'. There is a delicious piece of irony on Luke's part here, since his short stature meant that few had ever looked 'up' to him. Invoking a sense of divine appointment, Jesus says that he 'must' stay at the tax collector's house that day, and we read that Zacchaeus 'came down at once and welcomed him gladly'.

However long must that walk from tree to house have taken, I wonder? Even if it was but a few steps, it must have felt like a very long time indeed.

With each step, Zaccheus would have had to run the gauntlet of the angry and disapproving crowd. These were the people whom he had defrauded to gain his wealth, and they were in no mood to see him get star treatment from the Messiah.

In fact, I suspect it was the presence of the Messiah alone which made the journey possible. Only the presence of Jesus walking by his side would have made those hard steps past that hostile crowd possible. When Zacchaeus' dramatic change of heart comes about – pledging to pay back all those whom he had cheated four times over and to give away half his possessions to the poor – it is not quite clear whether it happens at the end of the walk, or at the end of Jesus' visit.

The path we tread when we know we are doing something which is right but unpopular can be a very steep and uneven one. We may find it littered with regrets and noisy with the sound of other people's opinions. Like Zacchaeus, we may find that it is possible to walk it only with an awareness that Jesus is by our side.

If you have a hard path to walk today, then stop and tell God all about it. Hold nothing back. Describe the way it looks and feels. Talk about the voices you can hear, both without and within. Then walk it anyway.

Prayer

> Dear God, today I ask you to walk by my side along this rocky and uneven path. Help me to hear the sound of your footsteps beside me louder than I hear any of those other things. Amen.

Walk 76

Strangers Walk Off with a Donkey

As they were untying the colt, its owners asked them, 'Why are you untying the colt?' They replied, 'The Lord needs it.'
Luke 19:33–34

Be honest now, have you sometimes wondered what on earth God is up to? Have there been occasions where his plan seems to make no sense at all, even with the strongest imagination? In our better moments we acknowledge that there *is* a plan, but at other times we fail to discern any trace of it.

Put yourself in the position of a family living in the village of Bethany on the outskirts of Jerusalem. Yours may have been a small house beside the road, perhaps with an olive tree or two at the front. Tethered in the shade beneath one of them is your prize possession: a donkey. The animal is a combination of family car and pick-up truck for your small business. It is valuable and vital, and you have yet to try it out properly. Then one day two men whom you have never met turn up and start untying the donkey. As these men lead it to the road you call out, asking them what on earth they think they are doing. 'The Lord needs it' comes back the reply over their shoulders. As you watch them heading off down the road, and the figures of the two men and donkey round the corner out of sight, you realise that it never once occurred to you to query who 'the Lord' was and why he needed it.

It seems that both parties in this story were walking a walk of faith. The two disciples had to trust that the curious phrase 'the Lord needs it' would be enough to get them out of trouble and avoid their arrest for theft. The owner of the donkey had to trust that all would be well, without the faintest idea of what was going on. It would be lovely to think that curiosity took him down the road into the city later that day, and that he joined the heaving, jubilant crowd as they shouted out 'Hosanna' to a Saviour riding into town (Matt. 21:9). Maybe he even shouted out, 'That's my donkey!' but found his one voice drowned out by the shouts and singing of the hundreds. We shall never know.

What we *do* know, though, is that holding onto things lightly serves us well. Holding onto things, whether jobs, places or possessions, with a hand sufficiently open that God can take things *out* as well as put them in, is a good thing. Learning to watch things go, like the man watching his prize donkey disappearing around the corner, is a key faith-skill.

As you walk today, try to reflect on the things which God has given you – whether they be physical things like a house, or conceptual things like the status that goes with your role. How would you feel if God turned up at the doorstep of your heart today, like those two people untying the donkey, and said 'I need *this* now'? If you think it would be really hard, then a gentle walk is a good place to turn over that uncomfortable prospect in your mind. That way, at least if it does come, you will find yourself a little prepared.

Prayer

Dear God, I am really not sure how I would handle it if you took [whatever it is] away, like those two men took the donkey away. I want to be a person who nods and smiles at the phrase 'the Lord needs it' but I'm not sure that I am, at least not yet. Bless this 'work in progress' today, I pray. Amen.

Walk 77

A Man Walks with a Water Jar

As you enter the city, a man carrying a jar of water will meet you. Follow him to the house that he enters . . .

Luke 22:10

Years ago, just after my A-levels, I travelled around Germany with a schoolfriend. We moved from city to city by train. On arrival at each city, we would be met by new hosts for the duration of our stay. Since we hadn't seen each other before, and the ability to transmit digital images had not been invented, we came up with a signal to recognise one another. On stepping off the train, my friend or I would carry a newspaper of such gravitas and dullness that no teenager would be seen dead carrying it, let alone reading it! The technique appeared to work, and we were never left abandoned on a railway platform with no home to go to.

When Jesus arrived in Jerusalem for the final time, he was very keen to share a Passover meal with his disciples. It would be a Passover meal unlike any other, with Jesus washing their feet like a servant and talking about his impending death as he shared broken bread and poured out wine. As strangers to the city, though, they would need somewhere to share their meal. Wherever should the disciples look, in this teeming city, swollen to overflowing for the festival? Jesus had an answer ready, which involved following a man with a water jar.

He went on to explain that the man would lead them to a house where an upper room would be all set with a Passover meal ready for them. Like my folded newspaper, the man carrying the jar of water would have been an unexpected sight. Carrying water in that particular society was a job carried out by women. I would love to have been there when that man was given his job. Can you imagine how it felt to be told to do something so culturally awkward in the busy streets of a crowded city? Not only that, but the rationale for doing it was the provision of a Passover meal for a bunch of people he had never met. Sometimes it takes a huge amount of faith to do an apparently inconsequential thing that plays a pivotal role in God's plan. Every time you share bread and wine in memory of that Passover meal, you owe something to this man who played his part by carrying a jar of water through a crowded city. Though we know nothing of his name or his background, his were footsteps of faith.

Sometimes there is a little bit of bravado in each one of us that thinks if God called us to step up for some great task, we would find the faith and courage to do so. It would be tough, of course, but with a noble sigh and the prayers of God's people around us, we would manage. What about if he called us to do the small and unglamorous task instead? What about if he called us to take a small walk of faith and perform a small act of faith, which only he and we would ever know about? That might be a different thing entirely.

Try to spend some time on your walk today thanking God for all the people who have played a small but faithful part in your faith journey. You could ask that you might be able to play such a part too.

Prayer

Dear God, I thank you for those who have walked into my life as your ambassadors, bringing a word from you, or performing a task for you. As I thank you for them, I pray that I might serve among their number in the lives of others too. Amen.

Walk 78

Peter and John Walk to the Garden

> Peter, however, got up and ran to the tomb. Bending over, he saw the strips of linen lying by themselves, and he went away, wondering to himself what had happened.
>
> *Luke 24:12*

It wasn't supposed to be like this. This was supposed to be a slow, dignified and nonchalant walk, like a grown-up. When it came down to it, though, I couldn't quite manage it. It had been two months since I had paid the holding deposit on my new little house overlooking the sea. At the time, the building work had gone up only as far as the downstairs windows, and I could not wait to see the progress. I parked the car at the top of the building site, and began to walk down the hill. As my excitement grew, a walk became a trot and a trot became a run. Patience has never been a virtue of mine!

Both Luke and John record the story of Peter and John visiting Jesus' empty tomb. Luke simply states that Peter 'got up and ran to the tomb', whereas John has himself winning the race to it! Once there, he waits outside for his friend Peter to catch up, who is then the first to look inside and see the evidence of the resurrection. There is something so wonderfully natural about all this. After hearing Mary's scarcely believable account of a risen Jesus, they cannot bear to walk to the garden, but run instead. One of them is propelled by his eagerness to get there first, but then lacks the nerve to look inside without any back-up. It is a moment both of spectacular glory and ordinary humanity. By the time both had looked inside, they must have been breathless from both the running and the amazement.

We are so rarely breathless in our excitement at the deeds of God. We are more likely to gasp at the power of a waterfall or the majesty of a sunset than we are to lose ourselves in a moment of worship in church.

Some years ago, I ran a little piece of research via social media about where and how people had experienced 'awe'. Among the respondents, the majority had experienced it outside, rather than inside church. They talked about soaring mountains, magnificent vistas and the wonder of a newborn baby, but few talked specifically about the deeds or miracles of God. Perhaps we have lost the ability to spot them, or the inclination to get excited about them when we do?

Today, I would love to be so excited about God's latest act that I find my step involuntarily quickening. I would love to rush towards that next word or deed of God with all the pace and enthusiasm that carried me round the corner to my new house. As on that occasion, I would like to suspend all my concerns about dignity in the excitement of the moment. How about you?

Prayer

> Dear God, I believe that you are still in the business of miracles. I believe you are still breaking rules and confounding expectations. I also believe that I have grown dull in my ability to see all of this. Please wake up my senses as I walk with you today. Amen.

Walk 79

A Strange Walk to Emmaus

As they talked and discussed these things with each other, Jesus himself came up and walked along with them . . .
Luke 24:15

Have you ever had a walk where you were on 'autopilot' to such an extent that you reached a place with hardly any notion of how you got there? Very often for me, especially in times of grief and sadness, walking has been a kind of therapy. It is as if I can expel the pain from my heart through the soles of my feet. When I walk in that way, it is very rarely with a destination in mind. Rather, I simply walk in the hopes that the rhythm of my feet on the grass or the pavement will drown out other noises within.

Maybe that was the case for Cleopas and his companion as they made their way back from Jerusalem to Emmaus on the first Easter Day. Maybe they were hoping that the seven-mile walk would put some distance between them and the bitter disappointment through which they had been, allowing their souls to recover a little. Along the way, we read, they had company. 'Jesus himself came up and walked with them'. Oddly, they could not see who he was, and instead fell into conversation with him, both expressing *their* disappointment and listening to *his* explanations. In the end, it would prove to be a transformative walk. At the meal which followed it, the true identity of Christ was revealed, and two people who had walked disconsolately *from* Jerusalem would hurry back *to* it, full of excitement and hope.

Don't you sometimes long for just such a companionable walk with God? When I first came to faith, I used to sing a very simple chorus that encouraged me to believe that Jesus walked beside me every step of my life's journey. Of course, I still believe it now. It's just that sometimes I am unaware of it. Like Cleopas and his companion at the start of their outbound journey, I am inclined to think that he knows nothing of my situation. Not only that, but like them I can also be altogether unaware when he does show up, continuing my journey in a kind of bliss-less ignorance.

It is not clear exactly what made them aware of Jesus' company in the end. We are simply told that as he broke bread and gave thanks at the table 'their eyes were opened and they recognised him' (Luke 24:31). Was it something about his turn of phrase, or a specific gesture as he held the bread aloft and blessed it, I wonder? Maybe they had been at the Last Supper, and were reminded of it, or maybe they simply remembered other meals they had shared with him along the way? Whatever it was, every shred of doubt was banished, and they knew that Jesus had been with them.

Oh, how I long for that moment of revelation, for that glorious sense that the ordinary journey or the unremarkable place is transformed into something altogether wonderful by his presence. Give me the joy that follows, rather than the ignorance which precedes that moment, any day of the week. A revelation of God's near presence on an ordinary walk today would be quite something, wouldn't it?

Prayer

Dear God, please don't let today be another day where I walk in ignorance of your presence beside me. Let me know that you are there, however you may choose to do it, I pray. Amen.

Walk 80

Nathanael Walks with Philip

> Philip found Nathanael and told him, 'We have found the one Moses wrote about in the Law . . . '
>
> *John 1:45*

I was a very impatient child, which is probably why I have landed up being not the most patient of adults. When visiting a museum, which we did often in my childhood, I lacked the patience to stop and read all the information in those glass cabinets. Instead, I would rush off into the depths of the museum in pursuit of the biggest and most spectacular exhibit I could find. I would then dash back through the darkened rooms, past the lit cabinets, to find my parents and beg and plead with them in shrill tones that they simply *had to* see this wonderful thing which I had found. It must have been very annoying.

As John's Gospel gets under way, the circle of those who know Jesus' identity begins to widen. At first it was John the Baptist, then Andrew and Simon Peter and then Philip. Philip was privileged to have a personal invitation from Jesus to follow him on his forthcoming trip to Galilee. To have such an invitation must have been beyond the expectations of any faithful believer who was awaiting the arrival of the Messiah. The remarkable thing is that instead of dropping everything and following Jesus straight away, he diverts before the journey begins. Leaving his personal invitation from the Messiah hanging in the air for a moment, he walks off to find his friend Nathanael.

However long that walk may have been, every footstep was motivated by love and generosity. Finding the Messiah was too good a thing to keep to himself, and he simply had to share it. Truth to tell, that walk turned Philip into the world's first true evangelist – telling another human being that he had found Jesus. Nathanael tagged along with Philip, albeit with a degree of scepticism, and was astonished when Jesus knew his name and everything about him. Philip's selfless walk added to the number of the disciples that day.

I thank God for the Philips in my life. I thank God for those who have put their own plans on hold in order to share some of God's good news with me. They include the leaders of my youth group, the pastor who baptised me, the wise mentors who took time to explain things to me and so many others beside. Like Philip before them, they knew that God's good thing was an even better thing shared, and took time to do so.

Don't leave on your walk just yet. Instead, sit down with a pen and a small piece of paper (small enough to carry with you when you walk) and note down the names of some of those who have been Philip to you. These are the people who have put you first instead of themselves, taking time to point you in God's direction when you have lost sight of him. Take the piece of paper with you when you walk, and pray for them along the way.

Prayer

Dear God, I thank you for the people on this little list. I thank you for their kindness and generosity, which has blessed me in so many ways. I ask today that you would bless them too. Amen.

Walk 81

Nicodemus Takes a Night-time Walk

> Jesus answered, 'Very truly I tell you, no one can enter the kingdom of God unless they are . . . born again.'
>
> John 3:5–7

Earlier, I mentioned a boy in my maths class who would ask questions on my behalf. That was more than forty years ago now, but some things never change. As I have been writing this book, I have been attempting to learn Welsh. Ours is a small class, and I am one of the two oldest students in it. Nonetheless, I still hope that someone else will ask the questions so that I can get an explanation for things which ought to be obvious to me. My understanding is reliant on their courage in asking the question.

Nicodemus was a person who was supposed to understand the things of God. To be a Pharisee meant demonstrating an exhaustive knowledge of the Old Testament Torah and an aptitude to learn the vast body of Jewish teachings. Pharisees were the guardians of Israel's spiritual heritage and should have recognised the Messiah of God when he walked among them. Many did not, and others were secretly curious. One such was Nicodemus, whose curiosity about Jesus got the better of him. In John's Gospel we are told that he came to Jesus 'at night' (John 3:2) and asked him all about his teaching. In response, Jesus gave an answer that forms the backbone to our understanding of the gospel.

How did it feel for Nicodemus to sneak off at night and seek out this radical and dangerous teacher, I wonder? Did he pick his route carefully through the city, making sure that he was not being followed? At stake was his own reputation for orthodoxy and his authority as a religious leader. To get caught would have meant many awkward explanations, or even denials, in the cold light of day. Interestingly, the next time Jesus was being discussed by his colleagues, Nicodemus stood up for him, reminding them that no one should be accused without due process. You can read all about that in John 7:50–52.

There are times when we all walk furtively in God's direction. This may be because we feel unsure about the things we want to mention to him. We are on less than solid ground, and we fear that he may put us right. Then again, on other occasions the thing which troubles us is precisely that we *are* on solid ground. We approach God almost certain of what he is going to say, and that scares us! Either way, the figure of Nicodemus, slipping through the streets at night and looking over his shoulder, is not unfamiliar to us.

Before we pray, it is worth remembering that the impact of that night-time walk on Nicodemus was both profound and permanent. Later in John's Gospel, as we have said, he stands up for the rights of Jesus to be treated fairly. Later, after Jesus is condemned and executed, Nicodemus throws caution to the wind by openly declaring his allegiance and providing spices for Jesus' anointing. A little night-time conversation with Jesus goes a long way!

Prayer

> Dear God, like Nicodemus of old, I need to pluck up my courage today. There are things I need to talk to you about, and I'm not sure what direction they will take me in. Give me courage and honesty, I pray. Amen.

Walk 82

Jesus Walks Off Grid

> Then, leaving her water jar, the woman went back to the town and said to the people ...
>
> **John 4:28**

While I like to travel with others, I have always enjoyed travelling alone too. I love that special frisson of excitement when all the sights, sounds and smells are new and unfamiliar. Mind you, sometimes the excitement can get just a little too much, and you develop a kind of sixth sense, or instinct. I was speaking at a conference in the Indian state of Assam, and had an afternoon free in which to wander in the town of Guwahati. I was doing just that, and turned down a narrow side street in search of the best place to buy a cricket bat for my son. As I rounded the corner, a small crowd was gathering. There was some jostling and some raised voices, nothing more. However, my every instinct told me that this was not a place where a tourist should be and I beat a hasty retreat. This was a few years ago, but now I would have said that to go down that street would have been to go 'off grid'.

In chapter 4 of John's Gospel, Jesus goes 'off grid' in a spectacular way. He goes into Samaria, where the least orthodox of all Jews at the time were to be found. Not only that, but he approaches a Samaritan woman, who is on her own, to ask her for a drink. Had he had a press officer or 'spin doctor' on his team of disciples, they would doubtless have cautioned against this, advising that the 'optics' were all wrong. By making this approach he opened himself to all sorts of reactions, ranging from mild surprise to outright disdain. Nonetheless, he did it, and a wonderful explanation of his identity and the nature of faith ensued. He could see right through this particular woman, and knew all about her past marriages and the state of the relationship in which she now found herself. No wonder she thought he might be the Messiah.

There follows one of the most delightful pieces of amnesia in the entire gospel. So keen was the woman to share news of her encounter with the Messiah that we read: 'leaving her water jar, the woman went back to the town'. That water jar was the whole reason she had gone to the well in the first place. At great inconvenience to herself, she had gone there at noon, the hottest part of the day, presumably in order to avoid too much interaction with her neighbours and their unwelcome opinions about her lifestyle. All of that now seemed irrelevant, such was her amazement at her meeting with Jesus.

Oh, how I long to be like that. I am not sure I can ever remember an occasion where I got so caught up in spiritual things that I completely forgot the practical things I was supposed to be doing. What about you? Sometimes our spirituality is so tame. It is like a temperate climate, never reaching the chilly depths of winter nor the sizzling heat of summer. It is polite and measured, and often rather boring.

I wonder whether you would dare to ask God that on your walk today you might lose track of time? Could you maybe ask him to create in you such a sense of wonder that Jesus came looking for you (as he did when he went off grid in this story) that it completely takes over from your planned route?

Prayer

Dear God, I thank you that Jesus came looking for the 'wrong' kind of person and then made himself known to her. She must have been so overwhelmed. Please make me truly, spectacularly and recklessly aware today that you came looking for me. Amen.

Walk 83

Walking with a Bed

At once the man was cured; he picked up his mat and walked.
John 5:9

A few years ago, I attended a residential conference for preachers. There were a couple of hundred of us there, from all different backgrounds and denominations. On the second afternoon, there were elective seminars, and I chose to attend one on 'preaching and disability'. To my shame I can remember very little of what the speaker said during the first half of the session. What I can remember is the second half. All the delegates were put into pairs and given a wheelchair. We took it in turns to be either pushing the chair or riding in it. We tried getting through swinging doors, accessing toilets and navigating narrow pathways. What struck me most, which will be obvious to many readers, was the difference in viewpoint when occupying the chair. Even the simplest encounter felt different from down there, and I was frequently overlooked in conversations. The change in perspective was everything.

In our story today, we encounter a man who has had the same perspective for many years. For at least thirty-eight years, he has been unable to walk. Each day, he is carried to the pool of Bethesda, in Jerusalem, in the hopes that the healing waters might get stirred up, and that he might drag himself into them quickly enough to get healed. It never happens, and for years on end his daily view has been nothing but the passing legs of the crowd walking by and the occasional spectacle of some other lucky person getting healed. Finally, all that changes when Jesus stands before him and asks him if he wants to be well. He grants the man's request to be healed, and orders him to pick up the mat on which he has been lying every day, and walk home.

This was something he had never done before. Never before had he walked home from the pool. Never before had he looked people in the eye as he passed through the streets, rather than looking longingly up at them. Never before had he carried his mat, rather than being carried on it. The change in perspective was everything.

The longer we go on walking in faith, the more we lose sight of how radical the change has been within us. We forget that we have passed from despair to hope, from darkness to light, and ultimately from death to life. Like that man in Jerusalem, our world has been changed forever and for good by the mere word of Jesus. Do we remember how that felt?

On your walk today, pray that God would jog your memory in a spectacular fashion. Pray that he would remind you deep down about how much your life has changed since you heard the word of Jesus. Think of that man, going from lying, to standing and then to talking, and give thanks for the truly miraculous power of Jesus.

Prayer

> Dear God, I thank you that everything changed on the day when I heard your word. From that day onwards, I could walk tall in a way I had never done before, and today I ask you to bring that all back to mind. Amen.

Walk 84

Walking Away from Jesus

Many of his disciples turned back and no longer followed him.
John 6:66

This was meant to be one of those moments that you remember forever – the lighting of beacons up and down the country for the late Queen's Platinum Jubilee. Thankfully, I was living near to one of the beacon sites at the time, and so I made my way there as the appointed hour got closer. The crowds were enormous, and it took quite a while to nudge my car across the field to a parking space. Safely parked, the dog and I joined the crowds making their way up the hill towards the enormous mound of timber that would be the beacon when the moment came. Unfortunately, for us, it never did. Despite the absence of loud noises and fire at this point, the dog took fright. She turned herself round to face back towards the car, and would not budge another step unless we returned there. Sadly, we left the crowds, the anticipation and the unlit beacon behind, as we threaded our way through the darkening country lanes to head for home.

In John 6, we read John's account of Jesus teaching the crowds on the shores of Lake Galilee. As the implications of his teaching became increasingly apparent, so did the unease among many in the crowd. These were things which they could neither understand nor accept. At this point, John tells us that the crowd thinned out.

Whether it was a trickle or a throng, that group walking away from the lakeside must have been a sad one. Maybe they were new to following Jesus, or maybe they had been there from the beginning. Either way, their sense of disappointment that this would go no further must have been palpable. If Jesus was not the kind of Messiah for whom they were looking, then would they ever live to see *their* Messiah come? Of course, we have the privilege of knowing the answer to that question The one and only Messiah had come, and was standing there before them.

When we walk away from God, we always do it sadly, whether we are aware of that or not. At the time, we may tell ourselves that it is an escape, that we are opting for the greener grass on the other side of the fence of obedience. It is not so, and that is a lesson that we learn just as many times as we make the mistake. The fact that we can learn it many times, though, is a measure of the grace of God. Those who walk away may also walk back, like the prodigal son.

Is there an area of your life where you have found the near presence of God to be just too close for comfort? Have you kept quiet about it in your walks and talks with him, as you would rather not hear what he has to say about it? Walking away from him brings no benefits, whereas turning back has many.

Prayer

> Dear God, there have been times when I would gladly have joined that throng of people walking away from you – shaking their heads and tut-tutting all the way. Maybe today we could start afresh, and I could turn my footsteps back in your direction? Help me to do so, I pray. Amen.

Walk 85

Martha Walks with Jesus

> She went out to meet him, but Mary stayed at home. 'Lord,' Martha said to Jesus, 'if you had been here, my brother would not have died. But I know that even now God will give you whatever you ask.' Jesus said to her, 'Your brother will rise again.'
>
> *John 11:20–23*

Have you ever heard somebody in public life say that they are 'walking back' a statement or a policy? Generally, the term is used as part of a damage limitation exercise to prove that concerns have been heard. 'Walking back' is every bit as awkward as walking backwards can be dangerous. What if you could truly walk back, though? What if you could actually walk back and right a wrong?

The last time we met Martha, she was getting it wrong by doing it right. In a bid to be the right kind of hostess, she ended up being the wrong kind of disciple. You can find the story in Luke 10:38–42. At the time she gets a rebuke, albeit a mild one, from Jesus. On this occasion, though, she is the one who reaches out to Jesus in her sister's hour of need. Their brother is dead, Mary is absorbed in the depths of mourning, and it is Martha who must summon his help.

In John 11, we read that Martha meets him out on the road, some distance from the house. Any lingering awkwardness from their previous encounter seems to have gone. There is not the slightest mention of her previous harsh words nor her questionable judgement on that other occasion. Instead, she reaches out to Jesus in her need.

Isn't this the most wonderful reversal? Here is Martha, the 'practical one', talking theology. The very person who had got it so wrong before is given the opportunity to get it spectacularly right here. Martha quite correctly states the theology of the day about a resurrection from the dead at the end of all things, but in so doing sets Jesus up for one of the clearest and most powerful statements about the resurrection to be found anywhere in the Gospels:

> Jesus said to her, 'I am the resurrection and the life. The one who believes in me will live, even though they die; and whoever lives by believing in me will never die.'
>
> *John 11:25–26*

Maybe you need to 'walk back' on something today. It may feel awkward, or embarrassing or difficult, but it is far from impossible. In one sense, Martha's 'history' with Jesus was not a good one, but it did not stop her from talking to him here. In fact, the sight of her walking towards him brings only the best and most positive things. Go back to Jesus, right now, with the thing which you need to unsay or the awkward situation which you need to unravel. You will find both compassion and welcome there.

Prayer

Dear God, I feel like I need to rewrite the script here. Of course, I cannot unsay the foolish or faithless things I have said, but perhaps we could start again? All I ask is that you listen to me, in my folly, as you did with Martha. Amen.

Walk 86

A Short Walk for Judas

As soon as Judas had taken the bread, he went out. And it was night.

John 13:30

Some walks may only be a few steps, but you feel like you have travelled 100 miles. I can remember one such walk in the early summer of 2022. For the past three and a half decades I had been attending deacons' meetings in Baptist churches, either once or twice each month. This particular one had started with me observing to the deacons that my first such meeting had been in 1987. One of them commented wryly that he had not even been born back then! Once my part of the business was concluded, I packed up my things, walked out of the church door and into the car park. With those few steps, something irreversible had happened. Somewhere between the top step outside the church door and the bottom one into the car park, I had ceased to be a strategic church leader. In fact, after that I walked and walked and walked on that warm summer's evening, trying to process what had just happened.

When John tells the story of the last supper, it is full of tension and poignancy, as the realisation gradually dawns on the disciples that something drastic is about to happen. There can be no line in the entire chapter which carries such dramatic impact as the description of Judas leaving the room. The four words 'And it was night' carry so much weight between them. Judas' was a short walk that crossed a vast chasm.

Maybe you have been on one of those walks in the past. Maybe you are even on one now. You know that the steps of this walk will change everything, and each footstep feels as heavy as if you were wearing old-fashioned divers' boots. There is a heaviness both to heart and feet as you make your way. Remember, though, that the path on which you tread is not unknown to God, and never has been.

Oddly, though, even that kind of 'heavy' walk can all be in God's plan somewhere. No sooner had Judas gone out unto the night, than Jesus says, 'Now the Son of Man is glorified, and God is glorified in him' (John 13:31). This walk that you are taking today is maybe one you simply have to take. Of course, you might not be able to see its purpose, but that does not mean that it is without one. You just need to trust that God who holds day *and* night, holds you too.

Prayer

Dear God, I cannot believe that every footstep is carrying me so far right now. Each one takes me further from what is familiar, and closer to the unpredictable. Please assure me again today that you go before me. Amen.

Walk 87

Mary Walks in the Garden

Jesus said to her: 'Mary.' She turned towards him and cried out in Aramaic, 'Rabboni!' (which means 'Teacher').

John 20:16

It had been just a few days since my wife had died, and with that seismic shock, my world had changed. Nothing felt the way it should have done, and emotions were either numbed to the point of absence or stretched to the point of unbearable sensitivity. In such circumstances, there was only one place that I wanted to be on that crisp November morning – the cemetery where Fiona would one day be laid to rest. There was a sort of solace there among the trees and the granite markers for each life remembered. In that place of remembrance there was no sound but the crunch of my feet on the frosty grass and the birds in the trees. I *needed* to be there that morning.

On the morning after Jesus' burial, Mary Magdalene knew where she needed to be. Jesus had transformed her life beyond all recognition – driving out her demons and giving her a stability and dignity which she had never known. On this raw morning, with him gone, she had to be near what remained of him. Compelled by her love for him, she made her way to the Garden of Gethsemane on the hillside overlooking the city of Jerusalem. There, among the olive groves, there might at least be some sort of peace for her. With no one around, or so she thought, she made her way to the tomb. Amazingly, it was not her encounter with two angels which would prove to be her most memorable conversation of the morning, since somebody else was there. Turning away from the empty tomb, she walked towards another figure, thinking he was the gardener, and asked what had become of Jesus' body.

Realising at last who it was, she took another step towards him at this point, since Jesus had to tell her not to hold onto him. Instead, he gave her instructions to go and break the good news to his disciples, which she did.

Can there ever have been a more transformative few paces than those which took Mary from the doorway of the tomb to the feet of Jesus? Within the space of those few steps, her hope was restored and her shattered universe mended. That little walk, and the revelation which it brought, would change the rest of her life.

I long for such a walk again and again. I long for that walk which brings me to the feet of Jesus and shows me his true identity where I had not seen it before. I long for God to change my view of the world every time that I think he is hidden.

Wherever you walk today, let it be with hope. Let there be a spring in your step as you anticipate the presence of the risen Jesus around every corner.

Prayer

> Dear Jesus, show yourself to me today, even in those places where I am not expecting to find you, I pray. Amen.

Walk 88

Mary Walks from the Garden

> Mary Magdalene went to the disciples with the news: 'I have seen the Lord!' And she told them that he had said these things to her.
>
> *John 20:18*

I can still remember the record player in my parents' sitting room, when I was little. It sat in a neat wooden cupboard that my father had built, and underneath it was a cabinet with small brass handles, which held my parents' collection of LPs. To be honest, many of the classical concertos and operas that they favoured were of little interest to me as a small boy. However, whenever they took Prokofiev's *Peter and the Wolf* out of its sleeve, my interest was piqued. I loved the way that Prokofiev's music portrayed the nature and mood of each participant in the story. When the eponymous Peter first appears, his music is full of trills and lightness, as he all but skips into the forest. Later on, with the wolf in hot pursuit, it is a different story.

In our story today, there is a similar contrast. Jesus has been in the tomb for just a few short hours, and with the first light of day, a woman comes to the garden to look for him. Mary Magdalene's life had been changed forever by the words and the grace of Jesus. At his command, the demons that had taunted her for years were gone, and she could walk tall once again. Coming to the tomb was a bit of a hopeless quest, since a dead Jesus could no longer help her, but somehow being near his remains was what she felt she needed. On finding the tomb empty, she had told the disciples, but stayed beside its yawning mouth when they were gone. Where else should she be? An encounter with Jesus himself followed, where all her sorrow and hopelessness was replaced in an instant with the joy of seeing for herself that he was truly alive. Brief exchange over, Jesus sent her on her way to tell his other disciples what she had seen, and to remind them that he would be ascending to heaven very soon. At this, John simply records that 'Mary Magdalene went to the disciples'.

How different must the exit from the garden have been to its entry for her. I wonder whether her footsteps all but broke into a run, so keen was she to share the news that the deliciously impossible had happened and Jesus truly was alive? Then again, she may have decided to walk slowly, and savour with each step that the world was now a more wonderful and hopeful and beautiful place than she would ever have imagined. She would never get this particular walk of wonder ever again, and may have decided to make it last.

It seems to me that ours is an age that is rich in information and is so often poor in wonder. While we may know 101 things at the click of a button, how many of them can we ever *truly* know? Our butterfly brains flit from one tasty morsel of information to another, rarely stopping to wonder at them.

Wherever you are walking today, why not choose to go on the slowest route possible? If you can, select a route that gives you time to ponder some of those things that really matter. Having chosen your route, pick no more than one or two things on which to dwell as you walk. They could be light and hope, or mercy and forgiveness. Whatever they might be, let them be your silent companions on the journey today.

Prayer

> Dear God, today I would like to walk as Mary did from the garden – bowled over by your wonders and certain of your goodness. Please help me to do that, I pray. Amen.

Walk 89

The Disciples Walk to Breakfast

> Jesus said to them, 'Come and have breakfast.' None of the disciples dared ask him, 'Who are you?' They knew it was the Lord.
>
> *John 21:12*

Until I visited North America, the whole idea of going out for breakfast seemed pretty alien to me. However, after visits to America, and especially to Canada, I have to say that I am converted to the whole idea! A strong pot of coffee and bacon with maple syrup certainly took some beating in the old town of Victoria, British Columbia. I imagine such a breakfast would have tasted even better had I been working all night to 'earn' it.

In John 21, we meet the disciples at the end of a long night of fishing. Presumably, the events of the first Easter week had taken their toll on these men. With so many things to process, they had reverted to the world they knew, and gone out fishing all night. The trip was a fruitless one, and they decided to make for the shore with their empty boat. Unrecognised by the men, the resurrected Jesus stood on the shore and instructed them to put their nets down on the other side of the boat. A miracle ensued, their nets were full, and it was all they could do to get the catch safely to shore. On arriving, it was apparent that Jesus was there, and had lit a fire ready for cooking. 'Come and have breakfast', he called out to them.

Can there ever have been a more unnerving invitation to breakfast? These men would have walked up that beach thousands of times after their fishing trips, day and night. However, they can never have had a walk like this one. Here was a man whom they knew to have died, a man whose voice and face were so familiar to them, who was now inviting them to have breakfast with him! It may well have been that they wondered whether they were seeing things as their feet crunched over the stones. Presumably the sight of that same man cooking fish and then eating it would have reassured them that all this was very much real. The Messiah who had amazed them with healings, regaled them with stories and astonished them with miracles was now doing it all over again. They would need some of that surprise and amazement to strengthen them for the serious challenges which lay ahead. Every single one of them would lay down their lives for the gospel in years to come, and they must often have thought back to this remarkable meal, remembering the smell of the smoke and the taste of that freshly caught fish.

I believe that we all need to keep in constant prayer that we never lose the ability for God to surprise us. May the day never come when we simply shrug at an answered prayer or merely raise our eyebrows at some truly miraculous provision. If we grow hardened to these things, then the pores through which grace seeps into our lives get clogged up, and we are stifled.

Before you do another thing, why not ask God today that he might take you by surprise? Of course, you can't tell him how to do so, or that would defeat the object!

Prayer

> Dear God, how I would have loved to see the faces on those disciples when you invited them to breakfast. My prayer today is that I would never, ever lose the ability to be surprised by you. Amen.

Walk 90

Philip Walks to a Crossroads

> Now an angel of the Lord said to Philip, 'Go south to the road – the desert road – that goes down from Jerusalem to Gaza.'
>
> *Acts 8:26*

Years ago, I thought that joining VI Form would be the coolest thing ever. After all, they had their own block, they didn't wear uniform, and they even got permission to leave school occasionally on 'free periods'! My admiration was confirmed still further when one of the activities was announced for our first induction week. We were split into teams of four, and each team was then divided into two pairs. Each pair was dropped off in two separate locations around a village in the Berkshire Downs. Team A had a map telling them where to find Team B, and Team B had a map telling them how to find Team A. On meeting up successfully at the rendezvous point, they would be given instructions on how to find the final destination. There were quite a few teams where the first couple reached the rendezvous point with ease, but could not progress without their teammates. Frankly, there was a lot of hanging about.

Philip the apostle was a busy man. At the time of this particular story, he was making a huge impact by preaching the gospel in Samaria. Crowds were flocking to see him and to listen to what he had to say. In the midst of all that, God gives him a peculiar instruction. He is told to 'Go south to the road – the desert road – that goes down from Jerusalem to Gaza'. Desert roads such as that one are not places where you would choose to linger, even now. Rocks and sand are so bright as to seem almost white in the full glare of the sun. There is no shelter, and anybody waiting there is exposed to heat, dust and danger. Nonetheless, Philip does as he is told and sets off, maybe more in hope than expectation.

Do you find it hard when God gives you only part of a plan? Maybe he tells you to leave one job without suggesting another to which you should go. Maybe he calls you to stop one particular avenue of service without telling you what might take its place. As I am writing this book, I am in just such a situation. I was called to leave a role in which I had worked for more than three decades, and to move to a part of the country where I knew nobody. There was no clear plan, and no clear map of the way in which my life should go. Like Philip, I was simply told to 'take the road'.

Sometimes the footsteps which we take in an uncertain direction feel like the biggest footsteps of all. That said, they may also lead to the greatest blessing of all. At just the same time as Philip was walking uncertainly to the road, an important official from Ethiopia was travelling that same road in his chariot, puzzling over the prophet Isaiah's writings and wondering what they might mean. Nudged by the Spirit, Philip approached the chariot, explained the prophecy, brought the official to faith, and started a chain reaction which led to a church of many millions in Ethiopia today.

Prayer

Dear God, if there is something uncertain about my footsteps today, then let me at least be certain of you. If my destination is unclear, then let me at least be clear that you are by my side. Where footsteps waver, let faith be strong, I pray. Amen.

Walk 91

Peter Walks Off for a Power Nap

I now realise it is true that God does not show favouritism but accepts from every nation the one who fears him . . .
Acts 10:34–35

It took me far too long to learn the lesson that I was not indispensable. An elder in one of my churches had been on the same journey, and said that he had come to the conclusion that God was perfectly capable of running the world without him. I was 20 years old and running a church-planting team in a foreign country during a year out from university. One of my team spoke no French, the other spoke no English, and I spent every mealtime translating between the two. As a real-life prayed-for missionary, I felt I had to justify my existence, and by the time I came home for a break, I was exhausted. Expecting praise for my sacrificial service, I was taken aback when a much older Christian took me on one side and said to me, 'If you carry on like this, you will be dead by the time you are 30.' That certainly brought me up short!

For apostles like Peter in the early church, the pace must have been punishing in the extreme. They were constantly on the move, always in demand and frequently in danger. Not only that, but no one had ever founded a church before, and they were having to make it up as they went along. When Peter called in at the house of his friend Simon the tanner, and walked up onto the roof to pray, he must have been desperate for some time alone. One thing led to another, and before long a hungry Peter was asleep and dreaming while his lunch was being prepared. Thank goodness he did. That short walk up the stairs, and the nap which followed it, led to a dream which would admit Gentiles into the Christian faith for the first time ever.

That dream, and its interpretation, would change the course of history. It would affirm the place of the Gentiles in God's plan, underpin the church's wider ministry, and a line can be drawn all the way from it to the person now holding this book.

Do you need to get yourself somewhere today where you can hear from God? It may start with prayer, as it did with Peter, but it may lead to a rest, a sleep or even a dream. Whenever I took personal retreat days during ministry, I always scheduled a sleep into the day. For me it was all about making the absolute most of this time away with God, and that meant resting as well as praying. Pray this through on your walk and then try resting when you get back.

Prayer

> Dear God, so often I feel that I am too busy to stop. Even if I do stop, I am busy thinking about the things that must be done when I start again. Forgive me for the arrogance which makes me see myself as indispensable, I pray – and let my feet take me to a quiet place with you today. Amen.

Walk 92

Saul Walks into Damascus

Saul got up from the ground, but when he opened his eyes he could see nothing. So they led him by the hand into Damascus.

Acts 9:8

At the opening ceremony of the Olympic Games in Atlanta in 1996, few will forget the athlete who completed the final leg of the torch relay and lit the Olympic flame. It was the world-renowned boxer Muhammad Ali. Once the scourge of every boxing ring he entered, his phrase 'float like a butterfly, sting like a bee' was the trademark of his particular style. None of that was in evidence on this memorable night. Fighting a personal and very public battle with Parkinson's disease, Ali's few steps to the flame were clearly an enormous effort of mind and body. Each step seemed to command all his attention, and as one hand held the torch aloft, the other juddered at his side. Here was a changed man.

Whatever must people have thought, I wonder, when the city gates swung open to admit the Pharisee Saul on special business from Jerusalem? His reputation preceded him – a formidable scholar and a firebrand in the hands of the Jewish authorities. In his hands he held the power over life, liberty and death. And yet, here he was, led in through the city gates leaning on the arm of one of his travelling companions. Shaken to the very core, he was taken to lodgings in the city where 'For three days he . . . did not eat or drink anything' (Acts 9:9). Here was a proud man brought low.

I think we all struggle when our view of ourselves does not conform to the view that others have of us. In all my years as a church minister, people tended to see me as the 'stable' one, the person whose faith was rock solid and whose doubts were all but banished. In good times, I could almost carry the illusion off, but in bad times it was another matter. I can also state categorically that those bad times taught me more than the good ones ever did. I wonder whether Paul remembered those faltering footsteps through the gates of Damascus when he wrote to his friends in Galatia, instructing them to lean on each other and to 'Carry each other's burdens, and in this way you will fulfil the law of Christ' (Gal. 6:2)?

Today may well be a day when you are brought low. Ill health or mental burdens may well mean that you do not walk as tall as you would like to. Not only that, but you may feel embarrassed to sense the gaze of others upon you as you wonder what they think. Why not let God worry about that? He is no more surprised by your faltering footsteps than he was by Saul's stumbling ones. It all turned out well in the end.

Prayer

Dear God, this book is supposed to be about walking, but I feel that all I can do is stumble today. There's neither pride nor strength nor dignity in my steps today. Please walk with me, and let me be so aware of your presence that the opinions of others seems not to matter so much, I pray. Amen.

Walk 93

Ananias Takes a Brave Walk

Then Ananias went to the house and entered it.

Acts 9:17

As I mentioned earlier, I am in the process of making some faltering steps in learning a new language – Welsh. Once I had got my head around the fact that there are twenty-nine letters in the alphabet and learned the many complications of Welsh diphthongs, I started to enjoy the simple pleasure of unravelling place names. Many of them are still beyond me, but I can pick out the odd 'Red Wood Drive' or 'King's Road' if I try. They all seem so much more interesting than 'High Street' or 'Market Road' somehow.

Our story today takes place in a street whose name could not be more boring if you tried. The street cut across the ancient city of Damascus and was called 'Straight Street'. When the story starts, a very humbled man is in a house in that street. Less than a week before, he had been an emissary for the Jewish authorities – feared wherever he went, and on a mission to exterminate the followers of Jesus Christ. Now Saul of Tarsus is blind, afraid, lonely and too traumatised to eat or drink. Ananias, a follower of Jesus, has been told all about this. He has also been told that he is the man to go and pray for Saul's healing. It is hard for us to imagine the sheer terror which this must have struck into his heart. Ananias was on Saul's hit list, or at least would have been. A discussion between God and Ananias ensues, during which Ananias pleads his case, pointing out Saul's murderous behaviour. God prevails, of course, explaining that Saul is vital to his plan to take his gospel to the world. Ananias accepts his fate, and heads off to see Saul.

How tough must those footsteps have felt. Did he stop and think, just before he knocked on the door of that house in Straight Street, that he might never come out of it alive? Was there a sick feeling in the pit of his stomach about what his fellow Christians would say if they knew he was here, doing such a thing? This walk could have been his last.

Of course, we know that it was not. Thanks to Ananias, Saul regained his sight, received his commission to preach, got baptised and then began a mission which would eventually take the gospel to the shores of Europe. None of that would have happened if Ananias had not bravely put one foot in front of the other to do the unthinkable and seek out Saul the Christian-killer. I hope I can recognise him when I get to heaven, because I would very much like to shake his hand.

Take some time on your walk to pray for those who will need to take courageous steps for Jesus today. They might have to walk into their manager's office and confront injustice in the workplace. They might have to admit in that same workplace that they love Jesus in a country where it is forbidden to do so. Their footsteps, like those of Ananias, will demand every ounce of their resolve, but they will be helped by your prayers.

Prayer

Dear God, I thank you today for Ananias and others like him. Thank you that they have swallowed their own reservations about your will and decided to do it anyway. Give them great courage and resolve today, I pray. Amen.

Walk 94

Rhoda Walks to the Door

> **When she recognised Peter's voice, she was so overjoyed she ran back without opening it and exclaimed 'Peter is at the door!'**
>
> *Acts 12:14*

The 'double-take' is a stock-in-trade of any TV comedy. The principal character walks into an unexpected situation for which the audience have been fully prepared in advance, reacts one way, and then swiftly another. I remember doing one myself. My wife's birthday and mine were just two weeks apart, and in the year that we both turned 30 we were invited out in-between the two for a meal at a friend's house. Oddly, almost all our usual babysitters in the church were unavailable, but we thought nothing of it. After finally securing a babysitter, our host welcomed us at the front door, and then urged us to go in ahead of her, which felt a little strange. As we opened the living room door, there was an eruption of party-poppers and cheers. All the people who couldn't babysit were there in that room to wish us happy birthday! Had mobile phones been a thing at the time, I suspect our reaction might have gone viral.

In Acts 12, Peter was in trouble. King Herod had already arrested James, the brother of John, and found his popularity ratings soaring when he put him to death. Now Peter was in prison and awaiting a similar fate. The church gathered to pray, and God heard their prayers – sending an angel to release Peter from prison. Arriving at the house where the church was praying, Peter knocked on the door, and a servant named Rhoda began a walk, or rather a run, which would place her into the history books.

To my mind, Rhoda's walk to the door leads to one of the funniest moments in the New Testament. She does a double-take and is too shocked to open the door to the very person for whose release they had been praying. Peter, who must have thought about the faces of his friends all the way from the prison, is left standing on the doorstep like a travelling salesman. I wonder whether Rhoda herself went back to open it, or whether the curious crowd pressed to the door? When at last it was flung open, there must have been tears and smiles all round, even for Rhoda.

Much as I smile at Rhoda, I also cringe at the memory of all the times I have been surprised by an answered prayer. Despite a lifetime of preaching and urging people to pray because God answers prayer, I still find myself bowled over every time he answers one of mine. Move over, Rhoda, there must be room for another on the embarrassed step!

Why not stop, right now, and call to mind some of the most surprising answers to prayer you have ever seen? It doesn't matter if they are old ones. It never hurts to say thank you again. You may find that these answered prayers make for very good company on your walk today.

Prayer

> Dear God, I thank you for Rhoda, because she could so easily have been me. Please remind me, with every footstep today, of all prayers which you have answered. Amen.

Walk 95

Paul and Barnabas Walk Separate Ways

> They had such a sharp disagreement that they parted company. Barnabas took Mark and sailed for Cyprus, but Paul chose Silas and left ...
>
> *Acts 15:39–40*

Years ago, a friend of mine was working his way through decades and decades' worth of church minute books. He was a keen historian, and loved such things. All in all, I was happy to leave him to it. However, when he told me that there was a minute in there recording a bout of 'fisticuffs' at a deacons' meeting over some minor issue, my curiosity was piqued. I never found it, although I am pretty sure it was there. Thankfully, I have never seen a physical fight in a church. That said, the occasional trading of toxic enmity coated in syrupy spirituality was almost as bad. Since we are all works in progress, none of us are perfect yet – and disagreements are bound to come.

Acts is an exciting book, as the gospel begins to spread like a fire through the ancient world. People from all walks and backgrounds are introduced to Jesus, and the fledgling church begins to grow as a result.

Not surprisingly, the toll on the travelling missionaries at the heart of this was considerable. They must have been frequently exhausted, and often in fear for their lives. Maybe disagreements were inevitable. In Acts 12, Paul suggests to Barnabas a return visit to the places where they had preached the gospel to see how everybody was getting on. He also wants to take Mark with them, who had previously stepped down when they were travelling in Pamphylia. Paul cannot agree to this, and Luke records their 'sharp disagreement'.

What an awful sight that must have been, to see such formerly solid partners walk away from each other. Barnabas had been the one to introduce

Paul to the church when they were sceptical that he had really become a follower of Jesus. Paul and he had been through great adventures together. How stooped their shoulders and how heavy their hearts must have been as they walked away from each other. The fact that God blessed their separate journeys does not detract from the sadness of this parting.

Reading their story now, I am reminded of every conversation that I have not handled properly and every relationship which has been wounded as a result. Parting on good terms can be a beautiful thing, parting on bad is anything but.

Before we pray about those partings, though, it is worth noting that this was not the end of this particular story. In the last letter that Paul ever wrote, 2 Timothy, he asked for Mark because 'he is helpful to me in my ministry' (2 Tim. 4:11). Thank goodness for good endings.

Prayer

> Dear God, there is a heaviness to my footsteps today, as I think of all the partings, both good and bad, that I have known. Right now, I place them in your enormous hands, and ask that there might be some happy endings. Amen.

Walk 96

Paul Walks Away from the Border

> So they passed by Mysia and went down to Troas.
>
> *Acts 16:8*

Back in the days where a phone was a thing on a wire connected to a phone line, ours was in a doorless cupboard that housed the washing machine. Depending on the privacy required, you could either lean *outwards*, towards the kitchen, or *inwards*, seeking refuge in the space above the ironing basket. This had been very *definitely* an inward call. I had just put a stop to what might have been such an exciting opportunity. Had I not made the call, I might have been on my way for a second interview overseas in a busy, thriving capital city at the heart of Europe. Instead, I had called a halt, knowing in my heart of hearts that as exciting as it might be to pastor such a church, there were things about it which meant it was not right for me. To go there would have meant going against my conscience, and that would not do.

Sometimes, following the apostle Paul through the pages of Acts can leave you almost breathless. From the day he came to faith in Jesus, he was commissioned to take the gospel to the 'Gentiles and their kings and to the people of Israel' (Acts 9:15) and he showed no signs of letting up. In every town, city and province he seized every opportunity to preach the gospel, no matter how hostile the reception. All of this makes it seem particularly bizarre when Luke tells us that 'Paul and his companions' had been 'kept by the Holy Spirit' (Acts 16:6) from preaching in the strategically important province of Asia. Trying a different tack, Paul attempted to go into Bithynia too, but was similarly rebuffed. After this, Luke tells us that they bypassed Mysia altogether and went to Troas instead.

We now know that Troas would be Paul's jump-off point for the journey to Macedonia, but he cannot have known it. Instead, theirs must have been a disconsolate journey along the coast and into Troas, gazing longingly at the places which were closed to them. How many people were in those towns and cities, they must have wondered, who needed to hear the gospel of Christ? No matter how many it was, theirs was not the task to preach it to them. There must have been a lot of conflicting emotions on that walk, I suspect.

As often as I have struggled with the challenges with which God has presented me, I have also sulked at the ones he denied me. Unable to see the full picture, like Paul and his companions, I cannot see the point. Then again, maybe that *is* the point. He does have the full picture, and the call to be his servant is a call to trust him in all things, especially the ones I cannot see.

For good reason, we have mainly schooled ourselves to keep the sulks on the inside. After all, part of being a grown-up is knowing that you cannot always have things your own way. Nonetheless, there can be merit in telling God about them once in a while. He sees them anyway, and giving voice to them can be a help to you. Why not vary your walking route a little today, so that you can take a sulky walk with no one to see you but God?

Prayer

Dear God, you know that I am not always convinced about the path you have called me to take. Sometimes as I walk this walk of faith, I gaze across at the paths others are treading and I long for them instead. Help me to find more contentment in the journey you have planned for me today, I pray. Amen.

Walk 97

The Apostles Walk from Jail

At that hour of the night the jailer took them and washed their wounds; then immediately he and all his household were baptised. The jailer brought them into his house and set a meal before them . . .

Acts 16:33–34

Ever since I was old enough to handle one, I am rarely seen without a camera in my hand. They have gone through various incarnations – from a boxy twin-lens reflex, to a 35mm compact, to a digital compact and now to a DSLR. It is a hobby which I have enjoyed enormously, and I am thankful for the memories that it has created from all around the world. All the same, there are occasions when my inveterate photographic hobby has got me into trouble. On one occasion, I was working briefly in Serbia, and had a day off. Together with my fellow lecturer, we travelled into the city of Novi Sad for the day. After lunch we went for a walk along the banks of the Danube. Thinking to make my picture of the city's bridge more appealing, I framed it with a launch in the foreground, pennants fluttering from its roof. Unfortunately, the launch belonged to the State Police, and a burly policeman, bristling with weapons, came out to reprimand me. He confiscated our passports and we had a nervous wait on the riverbank while he disappeared inside to note down our details. When he came back, and handed them over with a gruff 'no photos' warning, we all but skipped down the towpath. The feeling of freedom when we had been envisaging the opposite was unforgettable.

In Acts 16, we read the story of Peter and Silas in Philippi. A day that had started so well with the healing of a young woman possessed by a spirit had descended into accusations, mob violence, a public beating and a night in irons at the heart of the local jail. God was not done yet, however, and at midnight the chains fell off, the doors sprung open, and a terrified jailer came to see what all the noise was about. Relieved that no one had escaped, he fell to his knees, asked Peter and Silas how he could be saved, and they told him.

What a bizarre little midnight walk it must have been – from the jail to a place where their wounds were washed, and then to another, where the jailer and all his household could be baptised, and then into his house for a meal unlike any other. Perhaps the candlelight reflected on their wet hair where each had come up out of the waters of baptism. Perhaps the faces of the apostles shone with the thrill of their escape, and those of their new friends with the joy of new-found faith. Of all the places where these apostles walked, there can surely have been no walk more memorable nor joyful than the steps from jail to house. Perhaps they remembered them when they took their last steps later on.

Maybe today's walk is not a joyful one for you – but can you remember one that was? When my footsteps, both internal and external, fall heavy, I choose to remember happier ones. I remember climbing the Sugar Loaf in the Brecon Beacons, my darling wife at my side. I remember walking up the steps out of the baptistry on the night I was baptised as a teenager, full of anticipation about the adventure that lay ahead. These were happy steps, and I choose to remember them when I am sad.

As you pray today, ask God to remind you of those times when your path has been through happy places, blessed by his presence and full of hope.

Prayer

> Dear God, I thank you today for those moments when my footsteps have been light and my walk has felt propelled by joy. If that is not how it is to be today, then I thank you that there are times when that is how it has been. Amen.

Walk 98

Paul Walks Next Door

> Then Paul left the synagogue and went next door to the house of Titius Justus, a worshipper of God.
>
> *Acts 18:7*

The distance was not far, two or three steps at most, but it felt like crossing from one country to another. The one I left behind was full of quietness, shadow and regret; the one I entered was full of light, noise, laughter and warmth. It was the anniversary of my wife's death, again, and I was bent double with sorrow, again. Everything around me seemed to remind me of her; and there was no solace in my home. The invitation down the phone to 'Come and have a meal with us' felt like a life preserver flung from the shore. 'Come on in' were the simple words at the door, and they made all the difference in the world. That short walk across the threshold went a long, long way.

I don't know about you, but I find the apostle Paul pretty intimidating. I have always thought that he would have made a terrible flatmate – rising before me to pray, coming home after me having done yet more street evangelism, and occasionally peering down his nose at some of my less holy expressions! In Corinth, though, things were going badly. In the end, they would go so badly that it would take a direct vision from God to prevent Paul from giving up altogether. He had tried his best to preach to the Jews of the city, but they were argumentative and abusive. He simply had to walk away. The walk was a short one.

I wonder whether Titius said 'Come on in' like my friend did at the door? Whatever he said, the offer of his hospitality, together with Paul's night-time vision, clearly did the trick. Despite the rocky start, Paul stayed on in the city for eighteen months, teaching and preaching. Thank God for the simple hospitality that saved a good man from floundering.

This is probably one of the shortest walks we have encountered in this book so far, and yet the difference it makes is enormous. Like my own short walk, it was one from despondency to hope.

I wonder whether you need to make a similar walk today? Maybe you need to walk to your door and let someone in who is in need? You may be uncertain of the value of what you have to offer them, but it could have a big impact. Then again, maybe you need to walk to someone else's door, admitting your need by doing so. Paul must have been a burdened man, to walk away from the synagogue and knock on Titius' door. It may come no more naturally to you than it did to me on that November night to admit that you need help, but it might be just what you need.

Prayer

Dear God, I thank you for the time that you cracked open the door of heaven and said 'come on in' to me. Is there a door I need to knock on, or to open, today? Amen.

Walk 99

A Walk on the Quayside

What grieved them most was his statement that they would never see his face again. Then they accompanied him to the ship.
Acts 20:38

Some very dear friends of mine used to work in a school for the children of missionaries. It was a wonderfully diverse community, with children from all different cultures and backgrounds, playing, learning and living together. However, it was also an environment with many challenges. As my friend explained to me, living in such a place you had to be good at saying goodbye. There was a constant turnover in the school as new people came and others went, either permanently or on several months of home assignment. I have to confess that it is not an environment that would have suited me. I am not good at saying goodbye, and rarely do it without tears in my eyes.

Acts 20 is one of the most emotive passages in the entire New Testament, and I have preached on it on more than one occasion at my last service in a church. The apostle Paul was on his way to Jerusalem, and keen to get there by Pentecost if possible. With no time to stop off at Ephesus, he asked the elders from that church to make their way overland and meet him in the port of Miletus instead. This they duly did, and he came ashore to speak earnestly with them. In doing so, he looked back on the qualities and content of his ministry among them, made it clear that they would not meet again, and commended them to God's grace in the trials that lay ahead. Sermon over, they all knelt down together on the dockside, prayed and then had a tearful embrace. After this, says Luke, 'they accompanied him to the ship.'

I wonder what went through their minds as they walked to the ship? Maybe they thought of all the other things they should have said, or found themselves wondering what life would be like without Paul to guide them?

Very often, the emotion of such a moment robs us of the power of speech, since there is at once so much that could be said and so little that can be said. I suspect that it was a rather quiet walk for all of them, followed by an equally pensive journey back to Ephesus. In one sense, they were on their own now.

It seems to me that God doesn't mind a quiet walk. His is the kind of company that does not always require spoken words. The great thing about walking in the company of our Creator is that he understands those things which are either too painful or too profound for words. He just knows.

If you have painful, difficult things that you need to share with God, why not walk them out instead of spelling them out today? To him, the fall of your footsteps and the beat of your heart will be as eloquent as any words could ever be.

Prayer

Dear God, there is such a knotted tangle of threads and emotions inside me today that I am not even going to attempt to articulate them. Maybe we could just hold them together as I walk? Amen.

Walk 100

A Prisoner Walks Free

After this I looked, and there before me was a door standing open in heaven. And the voice I had first heard speaking to me like a trumpet said, 'Come up here, and I will show you what must take place after this.'

Rev. 4:1

Have you ever noticed that in every movie where a person is released from prison, there is *always* someone waiting with a car to take them home? They never have to take the bus or the train. Not only that, but the person meeting them is *always* on time. They have *never* got the day or the time wrong. They have never pulled round to the wrong entrance or got stuck in traffic on the way there. I wonder whether it really works like that?

John was a prisoner on the Isle of Patmos, a small Roman penal colony in the Aegean Sea. Conditions would have been harsh, with no contact from the outside world, minimal rations, and no prospect of reprieve. Imagine his joy, then, when Jesus appeared to him in all his magnificent splendour with the keys of life and death jangling in his hand. As the initial shock began to wear off, he found himself listening to seven letters, dictated to some of the key churches of Asia Minor. After that, it was time for a walk . . .

John was seeing and hearing things here which no human being has seen before or since. If he had been able to think at greater length, perhaps he would have compared it in his mind to that other perfect place where God walked once before. Alternatively, he might have thought how the river with the trees down either side looked so similar to Ezekiel's vision of a restored temple centuries before. As it was, these things were all so spectacular and unexpected that the most he could do was to record them, rather than analysing them. The amount of thought and interpretation which has gone on since the first century has more than made up for any lack on John's part!

How good are we, I wonder, at just absorbing God's Word and presence and the breath of his Spirit without forever feeling the need to articulate it? We live in one of the most 'annotated' eras of human history, where people curate and annotate their lives through the lens of social media for all to see. Western Christianity is very verbally based, and we like to articulate our faith with words wherever we can. Maybe there is a place, though, for simply absorbing God's presence, without feeling any need to describe it, or even to respond to it. Could that be so?

Our prayer today is the simplest, and maybe the most profound, of them all.

Prayer

Dear God, here I am.

Walk 101

A Walk Home

Lift up your eyes and look about you; all assemble and come to you; your sons from afar, and your daughters are carried on the hip.

Isa. 60:4

My wife, Fiona, and I used to take a lot of walks together. They weren't serious hikes, just walks. Somewhere I have a book of circular walks along the River Thames path. Each time we completed a walk, she would pencil the date neatly above that particular route. The idea was that one day we would complete the entire path together. Sadly, it was not to be, and I have no appetite to finish the rest of the Thames Path alone. Every time I see a couple walking hand-in-hand I feel both a warm sense of love and a sharp pang of regret. That is not the way I walk any more. For Christians, though, the prospect of a walk continued, in a different place, is ever there.

Our walk today is one which has not happened yet, for any of us, but the book would be incomplete without it. There are many people on this walk – hundreds or maybe even thousands. At a time of dire national emergency, with Israel's spiritual heritage trashed and her pride destroyed, Isaiah the prophet is given a vision of a better day, when God's people will come streaming back to the restored city of Jerusalem.

What an inclusive picture it is. Sons and daughters and parents and children all come streaming back through the open gates of the city. People watching from the ramparts can see the long line of them stretching away into the distance as far as the eye can see. A God who said he would never forget them is coming good on his promise. I remember visiting an enormous church in Chicago many years ago, and one of my lasting impressions was formed on looking out of a church landing window on the night of a church service, and seeing a string of car headlights stretching away into the far distance. People were coming!

We all have people with whom we have walked but who walk with us no longer. We miss their conversation and their easy presence. We miss the unmistakeable sound of their footsteps as they fall beside us, and in some cases the feel of their hand in ours. We miss their comments on the sights of the journey, or their encouragements to complete it. In short, we miss them. The remainder of *this* journey is made more bearable by the prospect that we shall pick *that* journey up again one day when the time is right. When we do so, the landscape will be different, but so will the journey. Rucksacks will be unnecessary, since there will be nothing to carry, and the prospect of getting lost will be irrelevant, since all will be found.

Today would be a good day to dedicate your footsteps to the walk not yet begun. The Bible tells us very little about heaven, but a lot about the fact that those who believe will be welcome there. We know that pain and weakness and doubt and sadness will play no part in our experience there. I am greatly looking forward to that particular walk, and the company in which I shall walk it.

Prayer

Dear God, we miss those who have walked this walk with us and do so no longer. Today, we name them before you, and thank you for the prospect of walking further together one day. Amen.

Walk 102

As you will see, this last walk is looking a little blank. In the preceding pages I have picked out 101 walks in the Bible, but there are plenty more to choose from. There is Jesus walking to Calvary, for instance, or Lot's wife walking away from Sodom, before that fateful glance back over her shoulder. Within the pages of Scripture there are all sorts of men and women walking to all sorts of places for all sorts of reasons. Hopefully our 101 walks together have given you an appetite to go searching for these walks. They are like micro-windows opening onto the vast vista of Scripture. They help us to navigate that wide biblical landscape one footstep at a time. May God bless your onward journey!

Postscript: A Walk Continued

So, there we are, our walk is done. Except, of course, that it is not. When I first encountered church, it was through my local Crusader (now Urban Saints) group. We used to sing a lot of old choruses, including this one taken from one of Isaac Watts' great hymns:

> We're marching to Zion,
> Beautiful, beautiful Zion;
> We're marching upward to Zion,
> The beautiful city of God.[13]

For those who like their grammar, the present continuous tense is important here. We are *in the process* of marching, and we're not there yet. The word 'upward' is highly significant too. Our journey of faith takes us up a hill whose brow we cannot yet see. Until we can, we walk onwards and upwards in faith.

The whole notion of earth being 'down here' and heaven being 'up there' can be unhelpful. It has led to extremes of unworldly asceticism on the one hand or a devaluing of earthly life and society on the other. However, the notion of our journey towards heaven as an upward one can have some value. It suggests an effort involved in the climb, which is undoubtedly true. It also reminds us that this will not be a quick journey, since it is uphill. Furthermore, any journey which ends on the top of a hill gives a different perspective not only on where you have come from, but the rest of the landscape as well. I am looking forward to that view when I get there.

As we have seen, the Bible has a lot to say about a lot of walks. When I was writing them, I had no clear idea of the order in which they would be presented. Instead, I wrote each one down as it came to me. In the end, I opted for an order which reflected their occurrence in the Bible, for ease of navigation. To achieve this, I wrote the name of all 101 chapters on separate pieces of paper and rearranged them slowly on my kitchen floor. As I went up and down the row of pieces of paper on all fours, a picture began to emerge. As different as all the walks were, the overall picture is the same. Underlying them all is the notion of the 'upward walk' described by Watts above. We are told not only that we should walk it, but how we should do so. Paul writes to his friends in Galatia that we are to '*keep in step with the Spirit*' (Gal. 5:25) while John writes in his third letter that we are to 'walk in' 'the truth' (3 John 1:3). How do we do these things?

Continuity with the saints

It is important to remember that this is a path which is not walked alone. Writing to those who had risked ostracisation and worse from their Jewish friends and family by their loyalty to Christ, the writer to the Hebrews reminds them that they are not alone. Evoking the 'Zion' of Watts' words above, he reminds them that they are on their way to:

> thousands upon thousands of angels in joyful assembly, to the church of the firstborn, whose names are written in heaven.
>
> *Heb. 12:22–23*

The church is a ragtag collection of prodigal sons and daughters who have stumbled with glad surprise into the sunny uplands of God's grace. From there they go onwards and upwards, sometimes falling, sometimes rising, bearing each other's burdens and watching each other's backs. Christian, you are not alone.

You may recall from Walk 98 that Corinth was a tough place for Paul to be. He was rejected by his first audience, had to find temporary lodgings and nearly gave up until God spoke to him in a vision. It didn't stop there. After he had moved on, the church he founded in Corinth would go through numerous trials, many of them caused by each other. Wanting to ensure that they would stick at it in Corinth, as he had once been told to do, he wrote to them about temptation:

> No temptation has overtaken you except what is common to mankind. And God is faithful; he will not let you be tempted beyond what you can bear.
>
> *1 Cor. 10:13*

If the walk of faith is an arduous one, at least it is one not walked alone.

However, it is not just the company of those who walk with us that matters, but those who have walked before us. You have met many of them in the pages of this book. They are young and old and rich and poor and weak and strong – but like me and you, they have been on that upward walk. They have trodden this particular path before us. They have all done it very differently – some with tiny steps of faith, and others with huge strides of courage that leave us reeling. They have blazed the trail.

A few years ago, I had a church member who worked for The Ramblers.[14] There are many reasons why they encourage people to get out there and use the footpaths that are protected by law, criss-crossing the countryside. Some of them are to do with good health and enjoying nature. Others, though, are to do with legacy. By treading the footpaths and keeping the overgrowth down, you actually preserve those paths for the people who will walk them after you. This is how it works with the path of faith too. The kings and prophets and queens and fishermen and jailers whom you have met in these pages have all been treading down the path for you; so that you can follow it and others can follow you.

Not just feet, but heart

You may remember from the very start of the book my Scout camp dilemma about the exact nature of a 'stout walking shoe'. I never found the answer. What I have found, to my cost, is that shoes bought in haste are regretted at leisure. A snap decision in a shoe shop can lead to miles of uncomfortable walking, or even to injury. I know, because I have been foolish enough to do it. However, I also know that the best walking boots in the world will not enable you to complete a long walk if your heart is not in it. It is all very well to set out with a spring in your well-cushioned step when the weather is fine. When the storm comes and the gradient gets steep, your heart as well as your feet had best be in it, or you will abandon the journey for sure.

There are good reasons why Jesus says that the 'first and greatest' commandment is to 'Love the Lord your God with all your heart and with all your soul and with all your mind' (Matt. 22:37–38). Simply put, the walk of faith cannot be sustained with anything less than that going on in our very soul. Despite his many failings, David was a man described by God as being 'after his own heart' (1 Sam. 13:14) since overall he sought to serve him. The power of Jeremiah's prophetic ministry lay in the fact that it was seared onto his very heart, and that he spoke and prophesied from such a place. Much of Paul's relentless energy in the New Testament could be put down to his deep conviction that this mission had been placed on his heart by God himself. Conviction goes a long way, or enables us to go a long way.

Although it is many years ago now, I look back on my selection process for ordained ministry with a little shiver running down my spine. The questions were tough and the probing was relentless in every interview. The call was discerned and tested by experienced ministers, scrutinised by my training college, and then verified once again by the first church that called me. The whole thing was palpably exhausting, but not as exhausting as ministry would have been for someone who did not have a call. Many was the time in subsequent years when I held onto my calling only because it had been so thoroughly tested at the outset. Your heart and soul have to be in the journey in order to complete it.

Continuous adjustment

I mentioned in Walk 68 that I have been learning to pilot a glider while writing this book. When I am waiting for my turn in the plane, I love to watch some of the more experienced pilots soaring and turning 2,000ft and more above my head. It all looks so graceful and exhilarating. I dream of the day when I might be able to do such things, but it is a long way off just now. The first few lessons are much more mundane. There is no soaring, no banking and no turning for the novice. The first few lessons are all about the 'attitude' of the plane towards the horizon, and the only skill to learn is how to keep that attitude steady. I haven't got it yet – but basically it consists of hundreds of tiny micro-adjustments to take account of changes in the temperature and behaviour of the air. In this way you keep the plane level and proceeding in the direction that you want to take until told otherwise.

To 'keep in step with the Spirit' as Paul urges (Gal. 5:25) or to 'walk in truth' as John describes in 3 John 1:3 consists of a lifetime of such micro-adjustments. These may affect everything from our conversational topics to our choice of career and our bank balance to our shopping basket. Those who would keep their eye on that 'upward' horizon have to watch their 'attitude' and keep moving in the right direction without deviation or distraction. The walk of faith consists not of one decision to embark upon it, but 1,001 decisions to stay on it. Hopefully, some of our walks will have helped with those decisions and micro-adjustments, as we have watched others making good or bad faith choices along the way.

Today is the first day of the rest of your journey. If the journey of faith has been harder or slower than you expected up to this point, it does not matter. If you feel ashamed of how often you have been distracted, then you need do so no longer. The moment you realise you have been distracted is the moment you put it behind you. The path of faith lies open before us.

Care to walk?

Notes

Preface

[1] Rebecca Solnit, *Wanderlust* (London: Granta Books, 2022).

Introduction

[2] Richard Littledale, *Journey: The Way of the Disciple* (Milton Keynes: Authentic, 2017).

Choosing Your Footwear

[3] W.B. Yeats, https://www.scottishpoetrylibrary.org.uk/poem/he-wishes-cloths-heaven/ (accessed 23 October 2023).

Walk 2

[4] https://www.lyrics.com/lyric/21928040/Matt+Monro/Walk+Away (accessed 23 October 2023).

Walk 13

[5] Roland Herbert Bainton, *Here I Stand: A Life of Martin Luther* (Peabody, MA: Hendrickson Publishers, 2009), p. 105. https://books.google.co.uk/books?id=NFbHwGvbIO0C&pg=PA105&lpg=PA105&dq=-God+once+spoke+through+the+mouth+of+an+ass+luther&source=-bl&ots=o1y0GM0i4y (accessed 21 June 2023).

Walk 22

[6] L.A.T. Van Dooren, *Steadfast Continuance in the Fulness of the Spirit* (Carnforth: Latimer Pub Co., 1982).

Week 44

[7] https://www.britannica.com/event/Chile-mine-rescue-of-2010 (accessed 23 October 2023).

Walk 45

[8] The Covenant Service (p. 288), from *The Methodist Worship Book*, © Trustees for Methodist Church Purposes 1999, reproduced with permission. Can be found at https://www.methodist.org.uk/media/27631/mwb-covenant-20221121.pdf (accessed 24 October 2023).

Walk 57

[9] It still continues today in other countries: https://sim.co.uk/product/pastors-booksets-bible-commentary-in-hausa-or-english/?only_search_result (accessed 26 October 2023).

Walk 61

[10] Martin Luther, https://www.plough.com/en/topics/faith/discipleship/the-way-of-the-passion (accessed 20 October 2023).

Walk 62

[11] @canseecantsee_

Walk 67

[12] George Wade Robinson (1838–77), 'Loved with Everlasting Love', https://www.hymnal.net/en/hymn/h/284 (accessed 24 October 2023).

Postscript

[13] Isaac Watts (1674–1748), 'We're Marching to Zion', https://library.timelesstruths.org/music/Were_Marching_to_Zion/ (accessed 25 October 2023).
[14] https://www.ramblers.org.uk/ (accessed 25 October 2023).

Tales From an Under-gardener

Finding God in the garden

Richard Littledale

Richard Littledale invites you to push open the garden gate and join him as he discovers the joy of gardening.

A reluctant gardener, Richard took up 'project garden' to help combat the loneliness of bereavement, only to find that the physical transformation of his garden mirrored a real change in himself too. Follow Richard's journey through 52 tales and uncover what gardening can teach us about patience, humility, hope, fruitfulness and the abiding goodness of God. Beautifully illustrated throughout, each tale includes a gardening story, a biblical reflection and a prayer.

Whether you are an enthusiastic beginner or naturally green-fingered, this gentle and encouraging book reveals inspirational thoughts about life and God from the perspective of the gardener.

978-1-78893-220-2

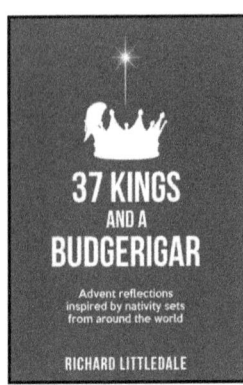

37 Kings and a Budgerigar

Advent reflections inspired by nativity sets from around the world

Richard Littledale

For many of us, putting out a crib set is one of our treasured Christmas traditions. But what do these scenes really tell us about the original nativity story?

Join Richard Littledale as he shares reflections, Bible readings and prayers for each day of advent based on his own personal collection of nativity sets from around the world.

Renew the wonder of the Christmas story through these thought-provoking devotions.

978-1-78893-158-8

Journey

The way of the disciple

Richard Littledale

'I want people to consider their life's journey, wherever their feet might take them, as a pilgrim's way – complete with leaving home, provisions, communications, distractions and a journey's end.'

In this delightful book, Richard Littledale helps us relate the concerns of the pilgrim's life to our own, and how this practice can help us walk a God-guided path. Enriched by the writings and artwork of other pilgrims, you'll be drawn along the trail, meet fellow travellers, have time for reflection, and find yourself changed by the journey.

978-1-84227-985-4

Postcards from the Land of Grief

Comfort for the journey through loss towards hope

Richard Littledale

Losing a loved one can be a lonely, isolating and disorientating experience. Written as postcards from this land of grief, Richard Littledale honestly shares his personal experience in an accessible way that helps fellow travellers to identify their feelings and find hope in the foreign country of bereavement.

Thought-provoking, honest, gentle and ultimately hope-filled, this is a helpful companion for anyone dealing with loss.

978-1-78893-071-0

Make It Grow!

Garden projects, prayers and fun facts to help you care for God's planet

Richard Littledale

Adults and children will love working together on these gardening projects that help us understand how to care for the earth and love our Creator God.

Each of these ten accessible projects have a list of things needed, a set of instructions, a small reflection, and a prayer ... with lots of fun facts to discover along the way!

So why not pull on your wellies, try these gardening projects with your kids or grandchildren and see how you can make a difference to our world?

978-1-78893-324-7

When God 'Buts' In

Finding strength to face the impossible

Kate Williams

Are you facing a situation that looks impossible?

Many biblical characters faced huge obstacles too, until God brought a 'but' into the situation that changed their circumstances in a powerful way.

When God 'buts' in he isn't meddling or interfering, he is divinely intervening in the situation. Whether that results in a miraculous turnaround in circumstances or grace to sustain you through a trial, God wants to 'but' in and be actively involved in your life.

Kate Williams interweaves her personal experience of challenge with biblical truth to help stir your faith and trust in God.

978-1-78893-308-7

The Power of Seven

*49 devotional reflections
7 biblical themes
Genesis to Revelation*

Emily Owen

Written in Emily Owen's unique, poetic style, this series of forty-nine devotions on seven biblical themes will inspire and gently steer you into a closer walk with Jesus.

Emily seamlessly weaves together reflections, prayers, personal stories and the encouraging 'voice' of God. Enjoy the world he gave you and stand together with him, with these seven themes as your guide: Creation, God *Is*, The Lord is My Shepherd, I AM, Echoes from the Cross, Add to Faith and Revelation Churches.

Be refreshed as you allow these powerful, thoughtful and imaginative reflections to point you to Jesus.

978-1-78078-990-3

Authentic

We trust you enjoyed reading this book from Authentic. If you want to be informed of any new titles from this author and other releases you can sign up to the Authentic newsletter by scanning below:

Online:
authenticmedia.co.uk

Follow us: